SPIRITUAL CAPITALISM
-and the 3 doctrines of power & money

ASGER FOLMANN

Copyright © 2018 Asger Folmann

All rights reserved.

ISBN: 9781791630317

CHAPTER 1

MYTHS

This is the Bible for the modern capitalist.

If you want success, you can have it. I sincerely believe that. But I also believe that most people haven't got the faintest clue about the magnitude of the necessary sacrifices. Success isn't something that just happens to people, nor is there a shortcut to it. Success is something that can be forcefully taken by the person who knows how to do so, and who is willing to deliver the needed sacrifice.

This book is written for those who wish to accomplish more than the trivial: those who seek extraordinary influence, wealth and success in business, art or any other aspect of life.

Let me start by killing a common misconception: if you're going to be extraordinarily successful, you will not simply be running a business. You will create and rule an empire. Let me also make it clear, that if you want to change the world, you need money. While it is possible to change the world one life at a time, as they say, this is a slow and cumbersome approach, which is frankly more telling of your current understanding of the world, than it is of your ambition to save it.

Consider for instance Mark who takes a degree, gets a good job, buys a house, settles down and starts a family. Throughout his entire life, he volunteers at homeless shelters, blogs about homelessness, shares news, posts about it on social media, and donates a portion of his income to organizations that fight domestic poverty. At the end of his life, he has probably made some sort of impact, although it is off course hard to measure the direct effect of his activities. Now let's compare Mark to Sarah, who starts out in a similar fashion. She gets a degree and a good job. But at some point, she decides to quit her job, and focus on making money instead of settling down. She makes millions on her first company, opens another one that makes tens of millions, and ultimately ends up with hundreds of millions. Although she hasn't spent a single day worrying about poverty and homelessness, she now starts exploring how she can help those who need help. In a matter of a few months, she is able to impact thousands, hire hundreds, create organizations that build shelters and houses for the homeless, and put pressure on politicians to change legislation to favor the homeless. At the end of her life, Sarah has improved tens of thousands of lives and her efforts even lead to a declining number of homeless people roaming the streets all over the country. And that's just her charity work. Her wealth may have affected even more.

Which of these people helped the homeless most? Mark, who joined organizations, volunteered in soup kitchens, donated his money, and spent his entire life as a social justice warrior? Or Sarah, who dedicated all her time, focus and energy to building businesses, and only a fraction caring about the homeless?

Monetary ambition is no crime. On the contrary, in fact. Each day, more than 5$ trillion shifts hands globally. If you died tomorrow, that money would still flow at the same pace every day. More importantly, if you don't make an effort to grab some of that $5 trillion, the people who are already wealthy will take most of it. Remember that, the next time you have the impulse to criticize someone for being greedy.

This is a well-kept secret, and it has been for millennia. From its earliest days, the Catholic Church has been preaching frugality and temperance, whilst in the same breath seizing more wealth than any one person would ever need. There's a reason why the royal families of pre-Christian Europe didn't like the church. The church was competition so fierce that the royals ultimately had to join forces with it to avoid extinction.

The same principle is in effect today, when spiritual leaders, politicians, and celebrities preach frugality and that "happiness comes from within", while simultaneously increasing their own wealth. I'm not suggesting this is a conspiracy, I'm simply stating that's how it is.

Most people who are looking to improve themselves are really looking for secrets and shortcuts. The main secret behind success, however, is that there are no shortcuts. The key elements of monetary success are sacrifice and discipline. Fast money is not a myth. In fact, it is the primary defining feature of success. Easy money, however, doesn't exist outside of the lottery and most lottery winners lose their wealth in a heartbeat.

On these pages, I will tell you the truth about financial success and, rest assured, it is harsh. I truly believe that anyone who has the motivation to succeed, can succeed. The problem is that many people think they are motivated, but when they realize just how much they need to dedicate themselves to something, they quit. That's not how people generally perceive it, though. It's easy to blame external factors beyond your control.

The fact remains, however, that success is widely determined by how much energy you are willing to allocate to acquire it. If you direct 99% of your energy and time towards success, you are highly likely to achieve it.

My own personal formula for self-motivation is to look at the whole thing as a game. Ironically, the minute I started looking at life as a game, I started taking it seriously. Life is not a walk in the park, and you are not inherently entitled to anything. Let me reiterate that. You have not earned the right to anything just because you were born. Society is happy to provide you with some basics, but anything beyond the trivial is something you must actively pursue.

The doctrines of power and money are the pillars of what I call *Spiritual Capitalism*. These doctrines are so profound that I doubt it's even possible to have success without them. In my opinion, they constitute the basis upon which all success rests. When I fully started abiding to them, I experienced the success of which I had always dreamed. But again, just a reminder: this is not a shortcut to success. It's a formula that works, but you must still do all the hard work.

You probably already know that there are two mindsets in the world. The first is the mediocre mindset, which at least 99% of the world population possesses. It is the mindset with which I grew up, and highly likely also the one with which you grew up. The rich aren't rich because they were born rich, although it may be easier to create and maintain wealth if you already have it. But without the right mindset, even billionaires lose their wealth. The true reason the wealthy are wealthy is that they've left consumerism, and joined the ranks of producers. This book explains in detail this first mindset that you must leave behind, and the second one that you must grow, nurture, and fully embrace to become a spiritual capitalist and achieve your wildest dreams. It sounds lofty, I know, but my approach is in fact very tangible and down-to-earth. It's not as complicated as most people think, but the sacrifice is very real.

Many people think that all they need is a great idea. They believe that if the idea is good enough, it will automatically spread, people will buy their product or service, and success will follow. Unfortunately, that is not true. You can have the greatest and most original idea, but if you don't reach people – and if you aren't capable of presenting it in the right manner – you will have no success whatsoever. When you hear success stories on the radio, on TV or on blogs, about so-and-so who invented this brilliant new gadget that revolutionized home cleaning, it is never a coincidence. A lot of time, hard work, marketing, branding, planning, and networking went into making that happen. The days are over when those things happen organically.

Other people focus almost exclusively on the spiritual mantras or habits of successful people. I read somewhere that mimicking the habits of successful people should be perceived as a prerequisite of success, rather than the cause of it. There's good reason to believe that's true. A person can have a psyche that's optimized for success, but without skills, knowledge, ideas, and other crucial components, they are unlikely to make anything of it. Others again focus on supernatural ideas e.g. the classic: *trust in the universe*. They don't realize that the basis of success rests in the human spirit – internally, inside you – not in external forces and agents. These people are, as I see it, pseudo-spiritual capitalists. In fact, focusing on external forces as determinants of success is the majority mindset. And if you do what most other people do, you must expect the same result as them: mediocrity. It's all about your preconceived notions about power, money and wealth. You must leave the majority mindset behind, and never return to it.

This book is not just another version of *How to Win Friends & Influence People, The Law of Success, Think and Grow Rich, The 7 Habits of Highly Effective People, Rich Dad Poor Dad*, or *The Secret*.

In fact, I am so critical of many of the most common ideas in the self-help industry, that I've dedicated an entire chapter to a systematic dissection and evaluation of them. You need to know what to pay attention to, and what to ignore. Even some of the reasonably sensible advice out there may be a waste of time for you depending on what stage you're currently at in your journey towards power and money. If you, like I, grew up with the idea that power is evil, and that it is, by definition, something that should be avoided, this is another idea you must leave behind. Power isn't inherently good or evil. Power is the same thing as influence, and you need influence, whether directly or indirectly, to reach your goals. Money and power is only evil in the hands of those that do evil. Unfortunately, they do a good job selling the myth that the rest of us shouldn't pursue it.

State of the Self-Help Industry

Today's self-help industry revolves around two main schools of thought: one that is based on supernatural ideas and concepts, and one that is rooted in scientific findings and empirical data. I call them *pseudo-spiritual capitalism* and *evolutionary capitalism*, respectively.

Pseudo-Spiritual Capitalists...

...make decisions based on their gut feeling.

...seek mental balance through divine inspiration.

...strive to improve their spiritual understanding of self and others.

...believe that humans are divine beings with a purpose.

...trust that the universe will provide.

Evolutionary Capitalists...

...make decisions based on scientific findings and statistical information.

...use scientific data to create codes of conduct.

...strive to improve their mental strength through self-instilled regimens.

...believe that humans are animals, who must decide their own purpose.

...trust in themselves only.

Both of these schools promote *some* ideas that are indeed helpful for entrepreneurs. The question isn't to which of these camps you belong. There's no reason for you to choose sides. My journey through life has led me down both these paths, – with and without the capitalism element. I have come to realize that not all self-help advice is equally conducive to success. Both schools of thought have something to offer, and both have elements that should be avoided like the plaque.

This book will not only help you distinguish between the good and the bad advice, but will also show you that sometimes it is justified to focus on the human spirit, and sometimes it is justified to focus on science and evolutionary capitalism. After all, the entrepreneur is method agnostic. Success is defined by results only.

Why don't I just get on with it and tell you the doctrines of power and money? Well, the reason why I dedicated a large part of this book to dismantling the most common advice is that, since you're reading this book, you're likely to read more books on entrepreneurship, and chances are you've already read several self-help books. It is, however, crucial that you are critical towards this literary genre. If someone who's had success writes a book on success, that doesn't guarantee that the book provides any guidance to similar success. If the author isn't exceptionally self-aware, he or she may very well attribute all their success to their unique personality, and while there's certainly something to be said about that, this can be very misleading. I could cherry pick single aspects of my personality, or events in my life, and attribute all my success to those aspects and events. But how do I know if that has even the slightest causal relation with my success? I don't, and that's my point. Most people consider themselves rational and logical, but the fact is that, when people analyze themselves, it is almost impossible to be truly objective.

Living in Los Angeles, I know many people who seek success, especially in acting and music. Many of these people struggle financially, emotionally, and career wise. Whenever someone finally experiences a bit of success, e.g. the first big role, or selling a track to be used in an upcoming movie, they often start saying the same thing:

"I believe we all have a purpose in life, and that things happen for a reason. There's a reason this is happening to me now."

They never said anything like that back when they struggled and couldn't even meet up for coffee, because they couldn't afford it. But now, all of a sudden, because they have a fraction of success, it's because the heavenly father and ruler supreme of the entire universe has taken a personal interest in them. Think about the absurdity and preposterousness of that. A starving actress struggles to land a role, but God notices her, and makes sure that she lands a supporting role in a Hollywood blockbuster that promotes sexual liberation, consumerism, and self-absorption. It makes absolutely no sense. But that person could easily write a book, attributing her success to just that. Advice that promotes and favors hoping, trusting, praying, and believing should be ignored. Almost, at least. More on that later.

How I Failed and Why I Succeeded

Before I delve into a dissection of good and bad advice, I must tell you how I succeeded, even though I did almost everything wrong. I'm not saying that my life was a failure per se, but just a few years ago I was a 33-year-old recently divorced academic, who had just graduated a masters program with anything but flying colors.

I had always had huge expectations for life, and throughout the years I imagined myself in many successful positions: a genius inventor, a prolific writer, a successful businessman, an accomplished actor, just to name a few. Sitting alone on my couch in the winter darkness of windy Copenhagen, I couldn't quite understand why I hadn't made it already – in at least one of these disciplines. I was on the verge of becoming resentful towards the world.

Why did I struggle to even find a tolerable job? How come I hadn't finished the novel I'd been working on for ten years? Why did people around me, who settled for so little, seem to have more than I? I couldn't quite escape the thought, that maybe I had played my cards poorly. And the clock seemed to be ticking.

But when I ran into an old girlfriend in 2013, a series of events were triggered that changed my life course. She invited me to come visit her in California, and even though I wanted to see her (I had a crush on her), I quickly realized that this was not just an invitation to come visit an old friend and fling. It was destiny stretching out her ethereal hand towards me, offering me a new life. Metaphorically speaking, off course.

I was at a pivotal juncture in my life, and I had to choose. I had been preaching to my friends for years that, "the greatest choice is to make no choice". I didn't know what I wanted in the US. Frankly, I had never imagined leaving Europe. All my friends and family was back there, and I loved the cool, Scandinavian hipster vibe in Copenhagen. But the realization that this was a unique opportunity, of the kind that almost never happens, made me consider my options carefully. In less than a month, I had packed up my belongings, terminated my lease, quit my job, and bought a ticket for Los Angeles.

Fast-forward five years. Today I live in a mansion with breathtaking views of mountains and Downtown LA in the distance. I am an actor. I usually play the bad guy in B-movies. But I've seen myself on the big screen. Occasionally, people recognize me on the street. I am financially independent. I'm not a multi-millionaire, and I dread tax returns just as much as the next guy. But I've made money, and I know how to make it. I compose music. Metal, rock, pop, folk, classical; whatever I feel like. A few of my songs have been recorded and released. They may not be masterpieces, but I like them, and I'm proud of them. I run two YouTube channels with thousands of subscribers. People that I've never met hate and love me. I run several companies. One sells expensive subscriptions to cryptocurrency market analyses. I receive dozens, sometimes hundreds of emails every day. People want to buy me lunch, invite me to events, collaborate with me, and offer me money to be featured on my social media. I am invited to speak at conferences all over the world. And oh, I'm married to the old girlfriend I ran into back in 2013.

Am I bragging? Maybe I am, but frankly, I'm only telling the truth. Life isn't perfect. Not even from my current vantage point. But it is pretty damn exciting. Comparing my current life to my old life back in Copenhagen, I can hardly recognize it. I have realized that nothing comes for free, and that almost everything you ever have, is something that you've earned in one way or another.

I'm not a superstar. I am neither Elon Musk, Brad Pitt, nor Dan Brown. But I do all the things I always dreamed of doing. And the things I work on are constantly growing.

I am not flawless. Far from it, in fact. But I posses one quality that brought me where I am today, and more importantly, it's not an ability with which I was born. That means that this quality can be taught. It may not be easy to acquire it, but it is simple. It is not the only piece of information you'll need to succeed, but without it, you never will. I will share this "secret" with you in the last chapter of this book, as it is the first and most important doctrine of power and money.

I want to give you much more than this one piece of advice, however. I need to enable you to implement the doctrines of power and money; otherwise they will hold no value to you. I don't just want to give you a piece of advice and leave it at that. I want to make you as prepared and poised for extraordinary success as you can possibly be after reading only one book on the subject. I want to write *the* best book on entrepreneurship and, therefore, I'm evaluating a long list of the most common pieces of advice given to entrepreneurs, so that you may know what to listen to, and what to shut out.

Separating Wisdom from Nonsense

In the next chapter, I will kill some of the most pervasive and persistent myths about success and entrepreneurship. In the same breath I will highlight the most solid advice and provide you with my own recipe for extraordinary entrepreneurial success: the doctrines of power and money. As mentioned, there are two main tendencies driving the entrepreneur self-help industry at the moment. One lends inspiration from the new age movement, whereas the other is inspired by science, psychology, and evolutionary theory.

I recently read a series of life-changing entrepreneur books. I was truly impressed with the quality of some of the newer works I read. And I was equally appalled by the quantity of nonsense in this space. Many books, blogs, articles, and videos are more confusing than they are helpful. It's one thing to find the right sources of information; it's another thing to separate the wheat from the chaff. Both can be challenging, and aspiring entrepreneurs can waste precious time finding their way in this jungle of wisdom and knowledge. The real danger, however, may be that some of the most commonly given advice is harmful.

There are many sub-genres in the entrepreneur literature. We will look at advice from growth-hacking, general self-help, classic wealth building theory, and the bizarre new age capitalism genre that seems to constitute the main part of contemporary literature.

The people who have the most influence give some of the worst advice. That is why there is a genuine need for a book like this. Some of the most ridiculous but diligently shared catchphrases must be dismantled, as these are downright detrimental to success. In the following, I therefore dissect the various slogans and advice, continuously provide examples from my own life, and deem each and every one of them to be either true or false.

If you read this book to its very end, you will not only belong to the 1% of people who are able to do so, but you will also learn my secret to success. I'm quite serious when I claim to have found the holy grail of success. Much advice is highly useful, but only one piece of advice is quintessential.

It should be noted that bad advice sometimes turns into something positive. I have not considered that in my judgments here. When I am critical, I don't mean to say that not a single human has ever benefited from the advice in question. I only mean to say that, for the overwhelming majority, that advice must be considered a pseudo advice.

It is very easy to be critical, especially of others, but true criticism starts with the individual taking a good look at himself. I've wasted years subscribing to much of the mainstream nonsense, and I have therefore learned what makes sense and what doesn't. It's simply much easier for you to read this book, than all the others. In other words: I wanted to write a book that could – at least in theory – be the only book you'd need to read on the psychology behind success. Dismantling pre-existing myths is part of that vision.

If Only I Knew Back Then

The inventor of the Mind Cheat Method, my friend Hans Jonas Hansen, recently told me:

"I wish I had read other books when I was younger. Now I'm reading the books I should've read back then, and the books I read back then, I'm finally ready to read."

Working on this book, it was tempting for me to organize the advice in two sections: one with good advice, and one with bad advice. I realized that this would be a bad idea. Things that stand out are per definition more salient, and are thus easier to remember. In other words: we ignore the trivial. Since it holds promises of neither danger, nor improvement, it is simply deemed irrelevant. By organizing the advice in a truly random manner, I increase the odds of you remembering more information from this book. Brain hacking 101.

As you will soon learn, much of the following advice can be good – if understood correctly – but the same advice may bring your demise if applied to the wrong situations. People generally think in a binary manner: good or bad. Pretty or ugly. Sad or happy. But reality contains a multitude of gray areas.

Just because an idea is condensed into one sentence, doesn't mean that it applies to all contexts. That is one of the greatest flaws of inspirational quotes, and of entrepreneurial advice alike.

CHAPTER 2
BUSINESS AS USUAL

Most self-help gurus have one thing in common: they've made the vast majority of their fortune from teaching people how to be successful, not by actually running businesses themselves. Although I have been mentoring people for over a decade, I have made the vast majority of my money from business. And perhaps more importantly, I've acquired most of my knowledge from running multiple businesses.

Many of these businesses were unsuccessful, but some were successful. During the past few years, I realized what I had done wrong in the past. These days, however, when people tell me about their business ideas, I almost experience a kind of "clairvoyance". I can immediately tell why that business idea won't be successful or what needs to be changed for it to be so.

The shortcomings of new businesses are almost always related to the psychology of the entrepreneurs trying to launch them. One thing that I've heard over and over again is this:

"I'm thinking about opening this online business that sells this digital product".

When people say stuff like that, I immediately know that they're not going to achieve anything unless someone or something disrupts them in their thinking. If you're *thinking about it*, you're thinking about it. That means that you're not doing anything beyond thinking. Thinking about something is completely unrelated to running a business. Even slightly more potent variations suffer from the same phenomenon:

"I'm working on a business plan for an idea I've had for some time."

This tells me two things:

1. You don't know how to launch a business. If you did, you wouldn't be working on a business plan, you'd be working on the business.

2. If you've had the idea for some time, then why are you still

working on it? Why haven't you launched it yet?

The devil is in the detail here. It *matters* what you're telling yourself and others. With that in mind, let's look at the 21 most frequently shared pieces of advice for entrepreneurial success.

1. It Takes Money to Make Money

Money can be made without money. History is rich with examples of that, although money can obviously also be made, if you already have it. What it does take to make money, is time. Money can be helpful, but it is far from the sole determinant of success.

Last night I wrote down the outline for a new business idea. I noted the various tasks that I would need to have done, how long they would take to execute, the skills needed to do so, and whom I would need to hire. I factored in expenses for supplies, services and contractors, and I was left with a rough estimate of how much it would cost me to open and run this new business. Around $6000 per month.

It was the draft for a lean startup. But it wasn't the draft for a bootstrapped *ultra lean* startup. Right before I went to bed, I realized that I would be able to launch the very same business, with only small modifications, for less than $1200 per month. I would have to settle for a lower quality product, but the quality would still be high enough to have value for future customers. I would simply keep everything on MVP (Minimum Viable Product) level. Instead of hiring a local copywriter, I would find one from a developing nation online. Instead of hiring a project manager, I would manage it myself. Instead of executing a marketing campaign, I would use my pre-existing network and see how far that would get me.

Are you cringing at the thought of this sloppy approach?

If so, you may have to change your mindset. Just as it is not a crime to make money, nor is it a crime to start with the basics.

Think of it this way:

Markets have a self-regulating mechanism. If a product is terrible below a certain point, no one will purchase it. If it's good enough to cover someone's need, however, you can spend the revenue from the early sales to improve on it and scale the business.

I have often seen people saving up before the launch of a new business. In most cases, these people become so afraid of spending any of their savings, that they end up only doing what they consider safe. But what is the safe choice for a startup? Is the safe choice hiring a company to build your website? Or to run your marketing campaign? Or is the safe choice to do it yourself?

Having money increases the odds of you spending more than you need to. It is nice to be in a position where you can always buy a service or hire another contractor, and I've done it many times. But did I really need to spend that money? In many cases, no.

Example:

I used to tell my friend:

"If only I had $1 million. Then I could easily make more money".

I have long since realized that I don't need a specific amount of money to start a successful business.

All I need is (a) knowledge and (b) time.

Every single day, when I read articles, books, or visit websites, I have the same, recurring thought:

"Wow, this could be turned into a business."

In other words: the distinct feeling that I can accomplish just about anything. The questions I ask myself these days exclusively pertain to: what kind of business do I *want* to be running, not what kind of business *could* I be running.

There is an underlying assumption here that we need to entertain for a brief moment. Did you notice it? I understand that, by keeping my eyes open, I will constantly stumble on new great ideas that could be made into profitable businesses. Get into the habit of asking yourself, "How could this be monetized?"

Sometimes the answer is, "It can't". And that's perfectly fine. But sometimes you'll stumble on new ideas, simply by pairing two things, that usually aren't paired.

When Hans Jonas Hansen and I talk, we always conclude:

"Yup, yet another business idea."

We both understand that many ideas can – relatively effortlessly – be transformed into a product. We finally have the knowledge to make it happen. I feel extremely privileged to have arrived at this mental destination. The journey here, however, was long and painful.

When I asked my friend, Liv Johannsen, CEO of the upscale fashion brand, Livness Inc., about her stance on this, she immediately replied that having enough money saved up before you launch anything, is extremely important. I'm mentioning this because Liv is on a very focused path. For her, it's all about creating retail distribution networks for her fashion brand. The way she does that is by traveling the world for business meetings and exhibiting at fashion conferences. This obviously takes money. Could she have tried to sell her top-shelf fashion line in an ultra lean startup manner? She could, but the point is that she's no longer running a startup. She has arrived at the stage where the most logical course of action is to spend money on these activities. Since she had the possibility to save up in a relatively effortless and not too time-consuming fashion (pun intended), that was the logical course of action for her.

In other words: I'm not saying that it's always stupid to save up money before you launch a business, a product, or a marketing campaign. I'm certainly not saying that you should always keep your operation as lean as possible. In fact, many serial entrepreneurs always start a new business venture by raising investor capital. Big money can certainly be used to make even bigger money. I am merely saying that, if it keeps you from starting in the first place, you have to ignore the fact that you have no money, and focus on developing an MVP.

It Takes Money to Make Money.

Verdict: false.

2. Successful People Make Mistakes and Learn From Them

Obviously they do. As do many other people who aren't successful entrepreneurs. That being said, it can be extremely hard to learn from your mistakes, and certain social phenomena makes it even harder for most people to learn from their mistakes – even from their own experiences. Festinger, who pioneered research on cognitive dissonance (having contradictory beliefs), stated that individuals who experience cognitive dissonance are likely to avoid social situations, where they might encounter uncomfortable beliefs. In other words, people naturally avoid situations from which they could learn. Not because their personalities make them more prone to do so, but because they are human. This is an example of an innate human tendency to which we are all subject.

In my youth, I was in the habit of blaming others for my mistakes. I didn't own up to them, and without owning your mistakes, you won't recognize them for what they are: *your* mistakes, and you won't be able to learn from them.

I once confided in an old coworker, that I was looking to get a divorce, because my ex-wife had cheated on me. He took on a thoughtful posture and, after a while, he said:

"Did you ever ask yourself, what it is that *you* do, to make your partners cheat on you?"

I became furious, thinking he was acting like a jerk, and left the room. I even told my budding ex-wife about the exchange, and we both agreed it was a crazy and insensitive thing to say.

But one day, years later, I recalled his words. I wondered if there was something to them. I realized that I might have had a tendency to rest on my laurels; that I might take my partner's happiness for granted, simply because *I* felt pretty happy. I also realized that this didn't only apply to relationships, but to most social interactions and situations. It suddenly became clear to me: there's an innate tendency in all human beings to assume that others feel and think like they do. When I looked into it, I learned that this idea is richly supported by research.

After having this realization, I made a habit out of reminding myself that others don't know what I know, and that I don't know what others know. The pervasiveness of this tendency is quite staggering, once you start noticing it.

In my experience, successful people are less afraid to take risks. Because of their unshakable confidence, they treat mistakes as learning opportunities. Common entrepreneurial wisdom tells us to (a) identify a shortcoming or a mistake you made, and (b) try to educate yourself on the topic, so you can improve next time you're in the same situation.

I, however, believe that a much more fruitful approach is to *understand that you are far from perfect*. It doesn't mean that there's anything wrong with you. Quite the contrary. You must understand that even the things you're good at can be improved. In fact, there's always room for improvement.

As William Shakespeare wrote:

"The fool doth think he is wise, but the wise man knows himself to be a fool."

This is the core principle that you must embrace in order to *truly* be able to learn from your mistakes. You must pound this mantra so deeply into your psyche, that it permeates your entire thinking. Once you've accomplished that, you'll be able to seek out new knowledge not just after having failed, but also to educate yourself constantly. Even small, seemingly insignificant, everyday events can and should be learning experiences. The journey starts with you realizing your own fallibility, regardless of your IQ, level of education, life-experiences, number of books you've read, etc.

I believe there's a widespread tendency – ironically among both the most and least educated – to think highly of themselves. The learned have read so much that they think themselves geniuses. Likewise, the completely unlearned don't know that there is an abundance of knowledge that they know nothing about. Both groups think they have it all figured out. This tendency may be caused by the fact that we constantly hear society telling us that we should *believe in ourselves,* be self-confident, and ignore our critics.

But consider this: who is the most self-confident person: he who has a vast knowledge and knows it? Or he who knows that he is fallible, and is fine with it? The answer is obvious, and the tie back to the Shakespeare quote should be equally obvious. It should be noted that the reason you need to embrace your own fallibility is that it makes it easier to absorb new knowledge and not take criticism personally.

Successful People Make Mistakes and Learn From Them.

Verdict: true.

3. If you Keep Trying, You Will Succeed

Albert Einstein is widely credited with having said:

"The definition of insanity is doing the same thing over and over again, but expecting different results."

This directs our attention toward the fact that "keep trying" is only a part of the equation. If you keep trying the same things over and over again, and no other part of the equation has changed, why should you expect a different outcome?

A few days ago, my digital marketing manager resigned with 3 days' notice. When I told my wife about it a few hours later, she sat down, looked compassionately at me, and said something to the effect of, "Really? Why? What happened?" As I realized that she was trying to accommodate the negative feelings I might have because of this, I also realized that I had already moved on mentally. I did experience a brief quantum of irritation, when I saw his email. But that was followed by my inner voice saying, "How do I find someone to manage his chores with such short notice?"

And by the time I told my wife, approximately two and a half hours later, I had long moved on to other matters, and almost forgot about the fact that my right hand had just quit. You may think that this is the reaction of a very cynical person. To that I must reply that I used to be an extremely emotional individual. To most people that has a negative ring to it, but back then I considered emotional sensibility a fine quality in any person. I'm not sure what happened, but here I am, 10 years, a divorce, two degrees, an acting and entrepreneur career later, and I'm simply not emotionally affected in the same manner by those sorts of things anymore.

Looking back with a positive outlook is inherently positive, and looking back with a negative outlook is per definition negative, and therefore also pointless. It doesn't mean that I'm not trying to learn from the experience. Obviously, I've asked myself how I can do a better job of motivating future employees and collaborators, but having a strong emotional reaction to this type of events is certainly not a good foundation for learning and improving in the future. Again, adopting a certain mindset seems to be key here.

What does this have to do with persistence?

A lot. All successful entrepreneurs understand that they must keep trying, even in the face of failure, but if you can reprogram yourself to not look at failures as failures, but rather as *unsuccessful attempts*, then you'll have a much easier time becoming a spiritual capitalist.

Obviously, you should keep the Einstein quote in mind, and don't just keep doing the same things, expecting new results. While perseverance is truly king, there are smart and stupid varieties of perseverance. I've had many business ideas over the years, I have often had to realize that it would be stupid to keep some of them going. In some cases, I had to face the harsh reality: that while my idea might be original, there simply wasn't a market for it. In other cases, I learned from the early mistakes I made: that the idea was great, but that I simply didn't have the time, money, and knowledge to follow through with it at the current time in my life. The main takeaway is this. Keep going, but don't be stubborn or fall so much in love with your idea, that you give yourself tunnel vision.

But what about J. K. Rowling, Asger? Didn't she just keep on going, even in the face of adversity and rejection? Wasn't she exactly so much in love with her idea, that her passion ensured her success?

Those are valid questions, but first of all, J. K. Rowling was not an entrepreneur. She was a single mom who struggled to get by for years, with only little time on her hands. Her novel was the only golden ticket she had at the time. True, she kept going and was extraordinarily persistent, and if she hadn't been, she would've never succeeded, and no one would've ever heard of Harry Potter. But we cannot know whether this is the reason she was successful. We could find tens of thousands of examples of people with similar stories, where the only difference is that they never sold their novels. I admire J. K. Rowling, but she must be considered an outlier, and fiction novels can't readily be plotted into success formula maps. Another way to look at Rowling's success is to simply recognize her commitment. There's a fine line between being interested in something, and being truly committed. There's also a fine line between believing in your own ideas, and not knowing when to quit. J. K. Rowling probably represents the extreme and rare outlier of what's sensible. And again, we're not interested in outliers: spiritual capitalists don't play the lottery, even though we see lottery winners from time to time. Outliers are the exceptions that confirm the rules. We are interested in that which can be formalized and used to significantly increase the statistical odds of our success.

When I asked my friend and fellow entrepreneur, Charlie Klarskov, about his perspective on this, he stressed that, even though plans are essential, the entrepreneur must also understand that things almost never turn out exactly as we imagined they would. This doesn't mean that you failed. In fact, had you not had a plan from the onset, you would've never arrived at your current destination.

The following homemade parable can be used to better convey the message:

An old sailor tells you of an exotic island with lakes of milk, rivers of honey, and hills of gold. For a shilling he agrees to draw you a provisional map on a cocktail napkin. You purchase a ship, and hire a captain and a crew. Using the shabby napkin map, you plot a course. After sailing for months, you finally arrive at the shores of a beautiful, tropical island, located exactly where the old sailor plotted it on the "mapkin". But alas, after two weeks of exploration on the island, you realize that there's neither milk, gold, nor honey there.

What do you do? Sail back home in disappointment?

Your original plan was to live off the milk, put the honey on jars, ship it back home, and sell it, and fill your ship's cargo space with so much gold that you would almost sink. None of those options will work, but does that mean that you should simply give up? After all, here you are on a beautiful bountiful island.

Couldn't you drink the water on the island? And weren't those coconuts you saw on the South beach? Maybe you could ship those back home for a profit? Or maybe you could open an exclusive resort on the island and use the tales of honey, milk, and gold to create a unique narrative around it?

I'm sure you get the rather crude and obvious point I'm making here. But what seems obvious when reading a childish parable is easily overlooked when facing a similar scenario in real life. This is the truth behind the statement, "If you keep trying, you will succeed". Whatever changed circumstances you find yourself in, rethink your original plan, and keep trying going onward. And again: sometimes the way onward means terminating your original idea altogether.

There are no guarantees whatsoever that you will succeed just because you keep trying, but if you don't, you're bound to fail. The advice should once again be perceived as a prerequisite of success, rather than a direct facilitator thereof.

If you Keep Trying, You Will Succeed.

Verdict: true, but...

4. You Must Work Constantly

Make no mistake about it: a lot of work goes into running a business, especially in its early stages. Perhaps even more so if you're running an *ultra* lean startup, where you need to keep running costs down and do most – if not all – tasks yourself. Not only are you doing the work but also you constantly have to educate yourself on how to solve various challenges, use software, write content in specific genres, etc. It is equally true that most people need to adjust their mindset dramatically, and accept that boatloads of hard work is in fact fundamental for creating any type of successful venture.

Spiritual Capitalists *are* in the business of making "fast money", but there is no such thing as *easy money*. There's more to be said about this topic than the obvious "be prepared to work your ass off", however true and important that is.

At the current moment I work 17-hour days, 7 days a week. Although it feels good, because I know it's part of a grander plan, it is not sustainable in the long run. The vast majority of tasks I perform at the moment can simply not be undertaken by a contractor or a partner, but every single task I execute serves the purpose of (a) bringing me to a position where I can outsource more tasks, or (b) adding more value to my brand and, therefore, also to everything I'll work on in the future. So while it doesn't immediately look like I'm working on creating a passive income stream, in essence, that is what I'm doing. I'm looking at the things from the big perspective.

In other words, I don't just complete tasks in a random order. I have, for instance, prioritized this book over other tasks for strategic reasons. I have not been able to bring all other things to a complete halt while writing this book, since I have certain obligations to my customers. But I've kept my work efforts at a minimum, in order to devote my time and effort to the completion of this book.

It is absolutely crucial to know *why* you're doing a specific thing, as well as *when* you're doing it and why that's important. Many people, especially so-called growth-hackers, have developed myriads of systems for time management and prioritizing. None of them seem to work for all, so we may conclude that individual differences play a role in what works for whom.

The perhaps most famous system for prioritizing appeared in Stephen Covey's *The 7 Habits of Highly Effective People*. In this extremely influential book, Covey suggests that we "put first things first", and distinguish between what is *important* and what is *urgent*.

Covey recommends completing tasks in this order:

1. Important and urgent tasks.

2. Important but non-urgent tasks.

3. Non-important but urgent tasks.

4. Non-important and non-urgent tasks.

This may seem rather abstract, perhaps even irrelevant, but I guarantee you the minute you start having customers, you will experience the pull between serving the needs and wishes of clients or customers, and what you should be doing in order to expand your business and focus on your long-term vision.

Practically minded individuals may be inclined to focus on urgent tasks, whether they are *important* or not. This is good for the daily management of your business, but it's *never* good to lose sight of the actual vision you have, which ties directly in with what Covey calls *important* tasks. Similarly, people who tend to focus more on the big picture may risk neglecting day-to-day issues when they arise and, therefore, run the risk of jeopardizing what they've already built. Some sort of balance must be found.

But remember: you *cannot* work constantly. You *need* to seek inspiration outside your office, and you *need* to see friends, and nurture romantic and family relationships. Why all the italics? Because I'm not saying that it's my opinion that you ought to see other people. I'm telling you that you *have to*. Unless you've managed to put your brain in a vat, or upload your consciousness to the cloud, you are a social being. Regardless of how introverted you consider yourself, you still belong to the human species. You'll languish if you don't see other people. Furthermore, you also need some input from the outside world, so you don't become 100% engulfed in your own micro universe. You are, after all, trying to create something that per definition will have a place in the world, and that others will adopt and with which they will interact. It's easy to become completely detached from reality if you're always alone with your own "brilliant ideas". Use friends and significant others as inspiration and air your ideas with them. When we are alone, we sometimes cannot see the obvious.

Some people believe that entrepreneurs should focus exclusively on results. When you work extreme hours you may find yourself in 'the zone', but you also put yourself at risk of mental tunnel vision, especially if you don't regularly share your ideas and plans with others. That being said, spiritual capitalists need to prepare themselves for countless days, weeks, and months – even years – of long hours and late nights. The goal may be to establish multiple passive income streams, but the journey there will very likely be long and windy. Brace yourself and accept the work that lies ahead. It's all part of the spiritual capitalist experience.

Forget about Tim Ferriss' four-hour workweek. While it is possible to create passive income streams and spend relatively little time on them, these are bound to be relatively modest in scope. No empires are built by accident. If your goal is to set up a few passive income streams and "see what happens", then nothing great will happen. You need to aim high and expect to miss your target. If you aim low, you certainly won't hit anything extraordinary.

You Must Work Constantly.

Verdict: true.

5. Ignore Critics and Trolls

First of all, there's a major difference between critics and trolls. I've had thousands of more or less aggressive comments on my YouTube channel over the years, ranging from spiteful criticism to threats of violence and death. Sometimes I've asked trolls to be a little more civil and respectful in their tone, and encouraged them to elaborate on their criticism. In about one third of the cases, I would get no response. In another third of the cases, I got yet another hateful comment. But in the last third of the cases, I got an apology for the tone, and an elaboration of what they actually meant to say. Many of these people have become my most loyal followers, and we have discussions that are high-level, respectful, and intriguing. It has become the norm for people to write things such as:

"I don't mean to be harsh, but I disagree with your statement."

I love that. I love the criticism, and I love the respectful manner in which it is served. The true trolls, however, I simply ban permanently from my channel. They are not helpful to the growth of the channel, they don't facilitate any debate, and there is little they can teach me, and I them.

I once ran into Danish actress, Sofie Lassen-Kahlke, who told me:

"You can get away with saying anything to anyone, as long as you say it in the right way."

Those words really stuck with me and have become one of my mantras. As long as criticism serves a purpose – e.g. to help you improve or educate you – it should be welcomed, regardless of what the intention was. This can be challenging in practice, naturally, but when you put yourself out there, you will quickly get a crash course in doing so. Many people struggle with this, since criticism is widely seen as personal attacks. Sometimes it is, but the hallmark of a spiritual capitalist is to not take criticism personally. Entire books have been written about this, and it took me around 10 years or so to transform a theoretical understand of it into something that actually allows me to listen to criticism without immediately shutting down emotionally.

For some people – maybe especially young entrepreneurs who have not yet fully developed a strong sense of self – it can be very hard not to perceive criticism as personal and negative. Ultimately, this is detrimental to your self-development and, therefore, also your success. Critics offer us free and valuable feedback. I don't always respond to criticism online, but in real life

I try to always make a note of it, and ask myself if the critics have a point. Trolls should be shut down and completely ignored, but not every person who looks like a troll is in fact one. On rare occasions, you may also encounter strategically placed comments that appear to be constructive criticism, but are in fact competitors or trolls that are out to get you for strategic reasons.

That being said, other people are the one major resource we have for learning, growing, and becoming more knowledgeable. Also, although the days of "the customer is always right" are coming to an end, sometimes we must consider and accept that public perception is more important than the objective truth.

For example, I've had many people accuse me of taking money to do undisclosed marketing on my YouTube channel. One person even made a video where he "called me out" for being paid to talk about a certain investment newsletter, by which he believed I was being paid. I follow a rather strict moral code on this channel, and I make sure to always tell people when I'm financially compensated to talk about anything. The person who made the video about me was blatantly lying, and his followers even thanked him for the heads up so they could avoid me. Annoying as it was, I weighed my options. I could ignore this guy, I could make a video where I responded to his false accusations, or I could sue him for infringement. I figured the two latter options would cost me somewhere between 10-100 hours and, therefore, decided to do nothing about this rather insignificant "influencer". It rubbed me the wrong way, because my sense of justice and reason had been violated, but a simple cost-benefit analysis of the situation and its possible outcomes made doing nothing the only truly rational course of action. Had the assault had serious consequences for my business or reputation and had it hindered my ability or compromised my credibility on a bigger scale, I would've probably made a different choice. But, as stated in the beginning of this book, the spiritual capitalist is building an empire, and an emperor doesn't respond to the manic outbursts of some rural chieftain, unless he sees the need to truly destroy him.

About 5 years ago, I was on the phone with an old friend who lives abroad. I passionately told him about an idea for an app I had just started working on. He listened and responded:

"It sounds like a great idea, but I don't think you realize how much work goes into creating something like that. It's not something you can just do."

I immediately took a defensive position. What did he know about that? Didn't he think I could pull it off? His words stuck with me.

I really wanted to prove him wrong. Not because of some narcissistic need to be right, but simply to prove to him, myself, and the entire world that, of course I could execute this semi-mad app idea – even on an extremely tight budget. I ended up hiring a team of app developers from India and, following my instructions, they designed one hell of an app. I spent around $5500 on it, as well as 2-300 hours of my own time. Ultimately, I lost interest in the project and more lucrative opportunities presented themselves. But the fact remains that I did develop the app. I never marketed it, Apple refused to list it in the their app store, and only a few people ever used it. But it was still a great idea, and I'm glad I did it, because I proved to myself that, by looking at a business as a game, it is much easier to pull it off. My livelihood didn't depend on the app becoming a success. I saw it as a lottery ticket. It was a game I played, and I enjoyed most of the ride, even though it was frustrating at times.

In a sense, it was good that my friend subjected me to his Scandinavian skepticism. It gave me an excuse to prove that I could do what he perceived to be impossible.

When I was around 30, I looked into meditation and practiced it for a while. One of the main takeaways for me was to accept the current state of things. Although I don't currently meditate, the realization stuck with me and, on most days, I tend to simply observe criticism – in real life or online – as if it has nothing to do with me. When you're subjectively detached from the criticism, it is easier to determine whether it has any validity to it. Never try to win an argument for the sake of winning it. It is stupid, frustrating for your conversation partner, and if they are at a more "advanced spiritual level" than you, they will certainly observe you, and find that you are less spiritually developed than they are.

As far as criticism is genuine – and by that I mean that someone thinks you could improve something that you say, do or sell – you should pay attention to it.

Ignore Critics and Trolls.

Verdict: false.

6. Always Aim for Perfect

"Perfectionism holds you back!" - Asger Folmann

The little voice that tells you, "This isn't good enough" isn't your voice. It is a voice that your mind creates to make sure you conform to *what you think it is the norm*. It is you being afraid of what others think of you. It's there for a good reason. Throughout past millennia, life was so hard that trying to get by on your own was virtually impossible. Bears, wolves, snakes, poisonous plants, aggressive mammoths, hunger, cold, frustrated tribe members, and psychotic monkeys all strived for our demise. We needed the social group to stay alive and procreate. We still do, obviously.

But will staying alive and procreating ensure your success? Obviously not. On the contrary, in fact. We are not hardwired to accomplish anything extraordinary. While it is only natural to seek the approval of the larger group, you will not be able to accomplish anything that has value on the marketplace, if you constantly orient yourself towards the norm. This can be extremely challenging for people to fully comprehend, the reason being that it is not something that happens on a conscious level. We rarely think, "I wonder if people will accept this?" or "Will they expel me from the group?" These are mechanisms that are so deeply ingrained in us that they are very hard to identify at any conscious level.

Even though it is certainly true that some individuals are less affected by what others think, we are all affected by what others think about us to some extent. I cannot count the number of times people have told me:

"I don't care what other people think of me!"

Really? Then why are you telling me? If you really truly didn't care, you would have no need to tell me or anyone else. What people actually mean is, that they are not afraid to go against the majority opinion, which is a valuable quality, but it is by no means the same as not caring at all.

If you decide to do extraordinary things, you can and must make a deliberate effort to rewire yourself, so you're not always hiding your fear of being judged negatively behind statements such as:

"That's me. I'm just a perfectionist. I like to be perfect."

Again, I'm not saying that you should live your life with a total disregard for other people's needs and safety, or that you should always release half-finished products and only focus on MVPs. Not at all. But I am saying that "perfect" is a concept that only exists in the realm of ideas – as Plato described it in his *Theory of Forms*.

Perfect is simply an illusion. Name me one product that couldn't be improved! Go on. No?

Good enough for the market is a step on the way, not the final destination. If you can release an MVP that is market ready, you'll start generating income, of which you can use a portion to improve on the product and create new products. Compare this scenario to one where you spend months developing an MVP. Then another couple months improving on it. Another month running it by a test group. Another month modifying it according to the feedback. Another month worrying if it's good enough. And then finally launching it.

That's almost a year spent on product development. But will you then be releasing a flawless, perfect product on the market? No. You will still face criticism by the first users of the product, and you will still spend just as long fixing it accordingly. In fact, you may even be more reluctant to implement customer feedback, since you already created "the perfect product". It is a counter-productive myth, that's being kept alive by parents and thought-leaders alike.

There may, obviously, be exceptions to this. In the blockchain technology space where I operate, launching an MVP that is too buggy can indeed kill a company, since the main value proposition here has to do with transfer of value and information in a safe and immutable way. Many companies have learned this the hard way. But if the core product is indeed market ready, then maybe your website and blog posts don't have to be 100% "perfect".

Truly unique and creative products are developed with little or no concerns about what others think.

Consider how art would look, if it were based exclusively on what the artist thought others would think. The best way to improve your product is by launching it and letting the market tell you what is wrong with it.

If I possess one personality trait that may have contributed to my success, it could be that I've never been a perfectionist. I don't like to turn in a half-finished product, but I understand that getting things done is much more important than them being perfect. Again, perfect doesn't exist outside the realm of ideas.

During my studies at University of Copenhagen, I remember a focus group interview I once took part in. The topic was something to the effect of, "What are the major challenges faced by elective students at the Faculty of Health Sciences?"

I still remember my amazement when I heard that every

single participant felt a constant pressure to perform. They all described the experience of not being good enough professionally, and everyone agreed that they felt a constant mental pressure to live up to certain perceived academic standards. They were very reflective on the subject, and most of them agreed that it was an internal, psychological issue they dealt with, more so than actual pressure being placed upon them by the faculty. When it was finally my turn to express my opinion, I confessed that I had no idea what they were all talking about. I simply didn't know this constant inner feeling of inadequacy they all described.

We all passed our exams later that year. My grades were average, where some of my peers had straight As, and others Cs and Ds. While my peers all had to learn not to be overly critical, I had to learn to be a bit more thorough – without adopting the self-critical aspect. And that is probably the main lesson here: learn to be thorough, focused, and effective, but don't be a perfectionist.

Spiritual capitalists need to arrive at a place where self-criticism is a positive thing. To most people, however, it's not. Personally, I am very self-critical, but my ego rarely suffers the slightest dent. Am I my own biggest critic? Not at all. I leave that to others, and they are happy to help me with that. In fact, I don't even have to ask for criticism; people provide it automatically. You need to find a balance where you're capable of producing products, content, or whatever it is you're producing, that has a certain level of quality, whilst not holding yourself back. If you're blogging, creating podcasts or YouTube videos, or writing songs, articles or short stories, you simply can't spend weeks on a single piece. If you do that, you will never be able to create the quantities of work that you need to, in order to build any kind of fan, follower, or customer base. The sooner you realize that, the sooner you will be successful.

Almost all great artists, from Beethoven to Lady Gaga, produced hundreds of completely unknown works of art, before finally producing something that struck a cord with the larger crowds. This is a profound realization.

I know countless people who describe themselves as perfectionists. But perfect is an illusion. Everything can always be improved. There is no such thing as the perfect product, the perfect dinner, the perfect holiday, the perfect woman, man, child, or animal. Perfection presupposes divinity and, regardless of your religious conviction, I'm sure you'd agree with me that divinity and business should be detached from one another. After all, there's probably a reason why you're reading this book, and not praying to the higher powers, that they may bring you success.

Always Aim for Perfect.

Verdict: false.

7. You Need a High IQ to be Successful

There are indisputably vast amounts of research indicating that IQ is the number one statistical predictor of success, at least in terms of vocational status and income. But that doesn't mean that people who aren't in the top tiers of the IQ scale can't be successful.

There is obviously also a potential logical fallacy hidden here. The fact that successful people have higher *average* IQs, doesn't mean that you're guaranteed success if you have a high IQ. Neither does it mean that you can't be successful with a lower than average IQ. It is a statistical observation, albeit a powerful one. Also, there are currently no techniques that have been proven to be able to raise people's IQ – although numerous companies claim otherwise – so there's really no need to waste time and money on IQ exercises.

It is also important not to conflate IQ with knowledge. High IQ individuals may have little knowledge, and low IQ individuals may have a vast knowledge on a range of topics. It may be somewhat easier for high IQ individuals to acquire knowledge, and their environments may have made them more prone to do so, but there is nothing to prevent anyone from educating themselves on relevant topics. In fact, a study by the University of Delaware concluded that people with an IQ of 115 or above can perform any job. But that doesn't mean that a person with an IQ of 115 will have an easy time performing any job.

Here's what you need to know about IQ and success.

Typically, various occupational fields are filled with people with similar IQ ranges. In one of his lectures, clinical psychologist, Jordan Peterson, said what I believe is one of the most profound things about IQ and success:

"You wanna find a strata of occupation, in which you would have an intelligence that would put you in the upper quartile. That's perfect. Then you're a big fish in a small pond."

What Peterson is saying here, is that instead of competing with a peer group that consists of only IQ superiors, individuals can place themselves at the top of the IQ pyramid by moving to a different field, where the average IQ is lover. After all, why would you try to compete with people of whom 90% are smarter than you?

This topic is a cultural taboo, at least in the modern Western world. We have all been taught that no one group or individual is better than another, and the idea that everyone should have *equal opportunity* runs so deeply, that the thought that some people are in fact – at least in some regards – better than others, is perceived as toxic and hateful. Another piece of evidence that civilization and culture instill certain misconceptions in us all.

But even though all humans share *the human condition*, we also have differences, and we would be fools to ignore that. This is especially true if it gives us an edge that most people don't have, simply because they are too ignorant or ideologically entangled to see reality. If you want to join the ranks of successful entrepreneurs – spiritual capitalists – you must be willing to put aside preconceived ideas in favor of scientifically demonstrated knowledge, however appalling it may seem to you.

Returning to Peterson's statement that we are far more likely to have success in areas where we would belong to the highest quartile (the top 25%), how can we apply this knowledge to our advantage? It can be hard to determine what the average IQ in a given entrepreneurial field is. But consider this example.

Let's imagine I wanted to make a splash as a famous chess player, touring the world, winning tournaments on all continents, and publishing memoirs about my most intense matches and the strategies I used to win them.

What would be my odds of succeeding with that?

Would I be able to achieve that goal using pure willpower, determination, and cunning?

Would money and a huge network help me?

Would the ability to manipulate others?

Perhaps so. But let's face it: I would need a high IQ to make that ambition come to fruition.

Chess is not a chance-based game, and the ability to think forward in time and anticipate the opponent's potential moves is key. This is solidified by the fact that no chess champion has been able to beat the best chess-playing computers since 2006.

Ironically, as I did research for this book, I stumbled on a post on Quora, where the author claimed to have an IQ of 140. He then went on to list his main priorities at the moment. Here's the irony: He clearly had no idea how to either start or run a business. He had already spent several years raising capital for something that in my opinion has very limited market potential. His calculations told him he'd be working another two years before he had enough capital to create a prototype. His plan seemed very single-minded and uneducated. He essentially demonstrated what I wrote a minute ago; that IQ and knowledge is not the same thing. Perhaps some high IQ individuals are at risk of ignoring expert knowledge, since they believe themselves to be so smart that they can readily figure out everything on their own. Research has also demonstrated that high IQ individuals are better at producing arguments, but only arguments that support their pre-existing opinions.

There are ultimately two major points to remember here:

1. If you're setting out to compete in a field that is populated with high IQ individuals, and if you're not in the high end of that spectrum, you may want to reconsider the industry you're in. You can, obviously, hire people with higher IQs, but you may not be able to pay their relatively high salary, at least not in early stages of your business.

2. Don't panic if your IQ score is below average. And don't rest on your laurels, if you're above average. Making money is widely a question of knowledge, much more so than IQ. The fact that high IQ individuals tend to believe themselves so superior that they don't need to educate themselves – e.g. on digital marketing – gives everyone a fair shot. Personally, I'm inclined to believe that motivation is much more important than IQ. That being said, understanding our own strengths and limitations is always helpful and is at the core of being a spiritual capitalist.

You Need a High IQ to be Successful.

Verdict: false, but...

8. Successful People Manipulate Others

My mother used to preach to me about how bad smoking was. That didn't keep me from smoking, and it wasn't until I started suffering from a chronic cough that I even considered quitting. That was in my late 20s. There is clearly something to be said about making your own experiences. Some things can be taught, while others must be learned the hard way. Obviously, my mother gave me a good piece of advice, but I wasn't ready to hear it. That makes it debatable whether it was good advice in the first place.

Similarly, an old coworker once manipulated me into situations that led me to realize that I was a *pleaser*. I ultimately realized that he was right; I *was* a pleaser, who put his needs below those of others. Ultimately, this led to a change in my life, and I managed to find a healthy balance between helping others, whilst tending to my own needs first. My mother's advice was well meant, and carried all the best intentions. My coworker's advice was sneaky and manipulative. He used NLP and covert strategies to manipulate me to take a closer look at myself. Evaluating which of those strategies brought me closer to success, my coworker takes the prize. At least in this specific case. Sorry, Mom.

Danish philosopher, Søren Kirkegaard, also addressed this topic:

"This is the secret of all helping art. [...] In order to truly be able to help another, I must understand more than he does – but, first and foremost, that which he understands."

Make no mistake about it: Kirkegaard was talking about manipulating people, so that they would be able to see "the truth". Shouting out to the masses from the top of your ivory tower never works. That also applies to entrepreneurs looking to sell their products and services.

Herein lies another profound realization: you are not your own target group. You need to *meet people where they are*, and that doesn't imply respectful equality, where you're both at the same level. It rather means that, in order to manipulate people (for a good cause), you need to understand where they are mentally. And if you don't know, you need to find out. This is pretty much the foundation for what in modern times has been dubbed *target group analysis*.

It is also the foundation for how many thought leaders conduct themselves: in an effort to "meet you where you are" they say things that they don't truly believe themselves. They use widespread myths and ideas to propagate their messages, because they know people will listen if the message resonates with them. In other words, they tell you what you want to hear.

This is crucial. Keep these two points in mind:

1. To truly rise to power in the world of entrepreneurs, you need to pay little attention to what you want to hear, but listen closely, when people say things you don't want to hear.

2. You must accept that running a business is ultimately about manipulating people. Not for nefarious reasons, but simply because it is an integral part of selling products and being successful. If you don't manipulate people to choose your product, the customers will buy your competitor's product. If you don't manipulate people to like you, they will like someone else, or even worse; they'll dislike you. If you are unable morally to defend manipulating people into buying your product, you shouldn't be selling it in the first place.

Social media marketing is pretty much based on taking whatever information the algorithms collect about your target groups, and then using it to manipulate them – at the highest odds – into buying your product or service. The sooner you realize that this is the name of the game, the sooner you'll be able to compete without putting yourself at a disadvantage.

During the dozens of phone calls I've had with potential business partners, many of whom are successful serial entrepreneurs, it has also become clear to me that anyone who's at the top of the power pyramid tries to manipulate you for their own purposes. I personally like to be completely open and honest about this during such conversations. I find that often yields the best results. About six months ago, for instance, I reached out to a company with which I wanted to collaborate. I knew the terms I would need in order for the collaboration to be attractive to me. Therefore, I told the company's chief business development officer, that I preferred to play with my cards completely open. I said I would commit fully to the partnership if, in return, they would pay me twice as much as they had suggested. She told me flat out that their concern was that they didn't know if I could be trusted. This led to a brutally honest conversation where we dropped all normal formalities. We ultimately closed a deal that was very beneficial for both parties. When I met the company executive branch in person later, it was like meeting old friends.

This is hardly manipulation, but I would never have closed this deal if I hadn't been aware of and addressed the initial manipulation attempts. In other words, when you communicate with veteran entrepreneurs or corporate executives, you must assume that they seek to manipulate you. If they pick up on the fact that you are oblivious to this, they will either succeed in their manipulation, or they may think you're too inexperienced to collaborate with. Manipulation attempts takes place at every level of running your business, from people writing you asking for discounts, to CEOs trying to trick you into signing unfavorable deals.

How far you'll want to go in your own manipulation efforts is really up to you. My personal take on it is to follow a moral code and a set of principles. As long as I stay within these boundaries that I've set for myself (e.g. never lie directly), I can't violate my moral principles, and I'll always be able to sleep at night.

Successful People Manipulate Others.

Verdict: true.

9. Successful People All Have the Same Personality Traits

After having read the section on manipulation, you may think that the best manipulators are unscrupulous sociopaths who care little for the well being of others. This couldn't be further from the truth. In fact, right after IQ, the personality trait, conscientiousness (defined as: *the way in which people control, regulate, and direct their impulses*) is the second biggest predictor of success, accounting for as much as 15% of all success – at least in a statistical sense. So when millennial self-help guru, Tai Lopez, tries to convince you to change your personality, he is actually on to something. Your personality is to a wide extent correlated with your statistical odds of achieving your goals.

Personality psychology is a huge field of study, and there are many interesting findings relevant to spiritual capitalists. To prepare you for your journey to stardom, however, I will focus only on the two best predictors of entrepreneurial success: *conscientiousness* and *openness to new experiences*. The openness trait is very often found in entrepreneurs and strongly correlates with creativity as well. It may not be a great surprise that people who invent new products or services are open to new ideas, but you could benefit from taking a personality test to determine how high your score is in this regard.

Conscientious people take obligations to others seriously. It is noteworthy that conscientious people are sometimes described as perfectionists, but I suspect this is a label the outside world puts on them, rather than an actual defining feature.

While the fundamental structure of our personalities doesn't change much over time (once we hit our early 20s), some personality traits can be tweaked. While I've always felt a responsibility towards other people (I used to be a pleaser, remember?), I also used to be extremely unorganized and spontaneous. When I took a *Big Five* based personality test recently, I scored very high on conscientiousness. When I took a similar test about 10 years ago, I scored very low. There are indications that we tend to change certain personality traits, when circumstances force us to do so. Since my circumstances have changed dramatically over the past 10 years, this could account at least partially for my change in this trait.

I believe that most entrepreneurs will automatically change certain traits, or aspects thereof, once they commence the journey down "the right path". You simply won't be able to run a sustainable business if you don't care about your obligations towards others. If your parents taught you this, good for you. If they didn't, the market surely will. Similarly, you won't be able to spend your time effectively if you aren't organized, structured, and oriented towards the big goals.

If you suspect that you may have low conscientiousness *and* low openness, you could take an online personality test to learn more. Choose one that's based on *Five Factor Theory*, or *The Big Five,* as they're commonly known. If you answer the questions honestly, and you find that you have a very low score in conscientiousness, you could consider finding a strategy to change over time. In my opinion, the best way to change is to simply grow the habit of observing yourself. Most people spend their entire life observing others but, if you observe yourself, you belong to a relatively small club of people who strive to become more self-aware. This is actually a good thing, regardless of the negative connotations commonly attached to the word.

Again, high conscientiousness and openness are probably not something that will bring you success in and on their own, but it may be hard to get much done with a very low conscientiousness. The real reason many successful people possess the same personality traits probably is that certain personality traits are defined by specific sub-traits (facets), which have to do with productivity, self-discipline, and the ability to think forward. If you learn to master those skills, you won't need to worry about personality tests.

Successful People All Have the Same Personality Traits.

Verdict: true, but...

10. Play the Long Game

After the cryptocurrency crash of early 2018, my business was severely threatened. Fewer people were interested in blockchain technology and cryptocurrency investments. My videos didn't get nearly as many views as before, and a lot of competitors had started new channels, basically competing for the interest of the few viewers still left. Add to that all the money people had lost, and there being no outlet for their frustration. My channel views plummeted, the value of my investments plummeted, my paying subscriber base plummeted, and to add insult to injury, my then virtual assistant sent out a devastating email to all our remaining subscribers by accident, which lead to the loss of another 30% subscribers in the course of a few days. My business was – in a strict financial sense – crippled. But I knew I was on to something. I knew I had built something of value, and not just fiscal value. I had just begun building my reputation in the cryptocurrency investment space. I had no intention to quit.

Be that as it may, I needed to pay my bills and my employees. I asked my friend, Charlie Klarskov, what he would do, if he were in my shoes. His response was:

"Can't you just do sponsored videos?"

He was absolutely right; that would solve my immediate problems. But it would be akin to peeing in my pants to keep warm. It would help for a brief moment, but it would hurt my overall brand.

Sure, I could pull in $10,000 a month doing sponsored review videos, but then I wouldn't stay true to my brand, and frankly neither to myself, since I would put my audience at risk of losing money. I don't mind doing paid reviews, but only if I can actually see the company I'm reviewing having a bright future.

I would jeopardize everything that I've worked close to 4000 hours to build. It made no sense. I knew that, if I kept my integrity, I'd be able to build something far more valuable. I was already doing it. Having less income was just a bump in the road. In other words, I focused on the big picture, and it's already paying of in terms of collaboration offers, speaking positions, and a general internal sense of satisfaction. In fact, I've turned down sponsorship offers worth hundreds of thousands of dollars. Building a strong brand is simply more valuable over time, than having a bit of traction here and now.

Playing the long game is crucial, but depending on the nature of your business, it can have different expressions. For instance, if your plan is to build a startup with the specific aim of selling to a pre-existing player in your field of operation, then your long-term play may only be a few years. But much can happen, and who knows, maybe that acquisition offer never ticks in, or maybe you end up loving your business so much that you don't want to sell it. Similarly, if your business is centered on you (as an author, consultant, artist, speaker, innovator, CEO, etc.), playing the long game is essential, since you are your own brand and it takes time to build and nurture that brand.

That being said, you should always define what the long game is. Are you planning on retiring on a tropical island in 5 years? Or 20 years? Or do you want your reputation to last throughout the ages even after the death of your physical body? These are important questions that pertain to the nature of your vision.

Any given week, I am forced to make hard choices between things that need to be done here and now, and things that need to be done for the sake of the long-term sustainability of my personal brand and my current business. More often than not, the counter-intuitive choice is the logical one. Take this very moment, for instance. My current to do list is 4275 words long. Many of the top things on said list are important to my business: I need to write and prepare the next issue of The Folmann Report (my cryptocurrency newsletter), manage forums, communicate with collaborators, manage employees, create content for my YouTube channels, attend auditions, and I still need to eat, sleep, and nurture my marriage. Yet, in this very moment, I chose to write this book instead. In a sense, I'm neglecting the obligations I have towards my audience. It may seem illogical. But this book ties in with my long-term vision, and right now I'm more motivated to write it than I have ever been. I keep my clients satisfied by checking in with them, and planning a stellar newsletter by taking notes, whenever I have ideas for it. But my clear main focus is writing this book.

Here's the dilemma: I can spend 17 hours a day managing what I have already built, managing a status quo. Or I can spend 17 hours a day creating something of value, and something that'll place me in a category I've always wanted to be part of: the author category. Add to that the fact that all the knowledge presented in this book really needed to get out. As with a cooker in which pressure has been building up for too long, it felt like a now or never type scenario. Right now, the book want's to manifest itself on these pages, but that could change if I wait too long. Momentum doesn't always have to do with external trends and tendencies: sometimes it's exclusively internal.

Focusing on the big picture – not the immediate tasks at hand – is a necessity. A cost-benefit analysis should always be made, of course. If writing this book now meant risking losing all my subscribers on YouTube, and all my paying subscribers, and missing an audition for the new Spielberg movie, it would probably not be a wise decision. But I am only human, and there are only 24 hours in a day, so I have to prioritize my time wisely. If I don't write this book now, when the words are practically falling out of my brain and down on the keyboard, when will I write it? And how long would it take me to do so at a later point in time?

Also, not formulating what you want and where you want to go is immensely dangerous. How can you expect to arrive at a destination, if you don't know where you want to go? For all you know, you could already be there, or sailing in the opposite direction, and you'd be ignorant in both cases. Having a destination in mind ensures that you are – at the very least – moving in the right direction.

And let me just reiterate my previous point: I rarely find myself at the exact destination at which I set out to arrive. But, at the same time, it's very clear to me that I wouldn't have arrived at this new place, if I hadn't had the original goal in mind. This is the nature of playing the long game.

Have a destination in mind. It should be ambitious. Plot a

course. After a while, orient yourself and determine if you need to adjust the course. If there's momentum to keep going in the current direction, keep going. Circumstances may change if you plot a new course, and we can't always make the forces of nature behave the way we want them to. If need be, you can always change your course later. As long as you're still moving towards your ultimate goal, in no more than a 90-degree angle, you're moving in the right direction.

Not having an ultimate vision is one of the most common shortcomings of entrepreneurs and, in most cases, it will lead to your demise or at least to the status quo. Playing the long game – and focusing on it on a daily basis – is the key to extraordinary success.

Play the Long Game.

Verdict: true.

11. Surround Yourself With Successful People, and You Will Have Success

Entrepreneur, author, and motivational speaker, Jim Rohn, is often quoted to have said:

"You are the average of the five people you spend the most time with."

Even though there is no scientific basis behind the number five in this statement, many studies have in fact demonstrated that we are far more influenced by our friends, than we intuitively think. Some research even indicates that we are affected in direct and indirect ways, not only by our own social networks, but also by the *networks of our networks*. That is: people you've never met affect you in multiple ways.

Scientists Christakis and Fowler found that people three degrees of separaration away from us still affect us. That is, friends of friends of friends, in other words. Although it can be debated whether these statistically observed correlations are in fact causal relations, it is still a clear reminder that the people we surround ourselves with are very important to our life trajectories.

Tony Robbins has stated that, "Proximity is power" and that, "You must get in the environment of the best of the best."

According to Robbins, that guarantees success. I find that somewhat preposterous and arrogant. Obviously, it would be helpful to have Bill Gates on speed dial, have Sunday brunch with Warren Buffet and Oprah, and brainstorm with the Dalai Lama and his most holy excellence, the Pope, over a cup of coffee. But unless you're part of the *invisible club* to which they belong, that is virtually impossible. It strikes me that Robbins has become so successful that he has completely lost touch with people who aren't as well-connected and rich as he is. Don't get me wrong. Robbins does seem to posses some unique and admirable skills in terms of reading people and identifying their "mental barriers". But for entrepreneurial advice, I will consult with other people.

Be that as it may, Robbins' statements do raise an interesting question: how can a startup entrepreneur such as yourself mingle with highly successful people? You can't, is the short answer. But what you *can* do is always be open to make new connections. I like to look at new connections as friendships. They may never evolve into actual deep friendships, but treating them as such ensures that you are authentic and live up to whatever promises you make them in the future. I also don't want to add people that I don't like to my network. I've met many powerful, famous, and interesting people on my journey over the past few years. Some are actors and directors I've met on movie sets, some are artists, others are financial gurus, and yet others are billionaires. Some of them I've wanted to befriend, but I know that most people they meet want a piece of them. You cannot expect to become friends with Elon Musk, based on a random encounter at a bar. Your motivation to befriend him and add him to your network is obvious. But what would his motivation be for befriending you?

I'm not a celebrity per se, but even with the relatively modest amount of success I have, I often get invites for lunch, free tickets to events, emails from people who want to meet or chat on the phone. I sometimes meet people who just won't let me go. I certainly don't mind all this. It's rather flattering, actually. But I simply can't deal with all the people who want to network and befriend me. My time is limited, and unless there's a special connection, or a potential tradeoff that helps me get closer to my long-term goals, I simply can't spend large quantities of time on random individuals. While they likely have an idea of how I can help them, I don't know how they can help me. Every once in a while, people approach me with concrete business proposals. Even though I decline almost all of them, I still appreciate this approach very much. Those people show me that they respect my time, and they are honest about their motives to reach out. I use the same approach whenever I'm interested in collaborating with someone. It doesn't always work out, but sometimes it does, and I find that most busy people appreciate that you get straight to the point. If there's a mutual benefit, this can turn into an actual friendship.

It is certainly true that the people we surround ourselves with affect us and that, when you commence your informed journey to extraordinary success, some of your old friendships may be hard to maintain. I don't suggest that you simply dump friends, however. Only that you let things play out in an organic manner. Time is one of the most crucial aspects of success, and you may find that some friendships simply aren't compatible with your new lifestyle. Others, however, may prove inspiring. A person doesn't have to be an entrepreneur in order to inspire you. As long as there is mutual respect between you, it'll work.

Some self-help gurus and coaches are very adamant in their stance on this. I'm not quite as extreme as Dan Pena, for example. According to him, you're an idiot if you're not the poorest person in your peer group. I personally have numerous people in my peer group that may be poorer than I in a financial sense, but whom I expect to be very successful in the future. That said, the people you surround yourself with *do* affect you, much more than you'd intuitively think, so it is something to which you should pay close attention.

One quality that I highly appreciate in friendships and business alike is the ability of your friends to ask you the hard questions. That means to really drill deep into potential flaws of your business or even your character. Instead of becoming insulted, use it as an invaluable chance to examine the darkest and most vulnerable regions of your personality. If you have a healthy psyche and a strong character, you are easily able to absorb criticism, regardless of how personal it is. Your friend is merely trying to help you improve, and since perfection is an illusion, there's always room for improvement. Have a dynamic growth mindset, not a static equilibrium one. Not all personal questions are insults, and not all people asking these questions are toxic people who you should avoid.

You probably have friends who are neither entrepreneurs, nor successful. But maybe you see potential in them. I find myself having become a sort of mentor for several friends who aren't actively pursuing the entrepreneur lifestyle, but who loudly express a desire for something more than the trivial. My friend, Mia, for instance, recently told me that she was fed up with her 9-5 job. When I asked her what she really wanted to do, she said that she wanted to change the world, that she believed everyone has a life-purpose, and that she wanted to help people find that life-purpose. When I asked her what she was currently doing to change the world, she paused. After a while she admitted:

"Not a whole lot."

By coaching Mia, I got to put some of my own advice to the test, and it has been extremely helpful for me to do so. It has forced me to articulate my knowledge and put it into formulas. Other friends will meet you with resentfulness. Those are typically your highest IQ friends who, for various reasons, never got around to creating their own success, perhaps because they assume that their intellect is enough to persevere. Change starts by formulating what it is you want to do. What you want to make of your life. Who you want to be, essentially. And this is why whom you surround yourself with is crucial.

How do you join the aforementioned invisible club?

When you are successful in your niche, people will start reaching out to you. As soon as you take the decision to make something extraordinary out of your life, you already belong to *a* new club. It is not the club that Tony Robbins tells you to join, but it is a club of people who are all on the path to break free of mediocrity: the club of entrepreneurs. This club has hundreds of thousands of members globally, and many of them will fail. Some of them won't, however, but if you've followed each other's journeys, you can likely call some of those people your friends. There are plenty of online communities for entrepreneurs, and those places can prove to be a valuable source of advice and support. I've been writing and participating in such groups for over 10 years, and most people in those communities are genuinely eager to help each other succeed.

This is how I've made most of my professional connections: I've constantly befriended entrepreneurs who (a) I like, and (b) are at various stages of rolling out their businesses. If I get the sense that people are trying to use me for some undisclosed agenda, I simply tell them. Some are still in the conceptual phase; others already run companies worth a several million dollars. Some are in my industry, others are in adjacent fields. I typically collaborate with people running blockchain companies. They need me to spread awareness about their companies and I need then, since the topic of my main YouTube channel is cryptocurrencies. Sometimes these collaborations are strictly monetary – i.e. companies pay me for promotion – but sometimes we are motivated by aligned values in a more general sense. In the case of the latter, I mention them on my channel, and they use their network to give me exposure on radio shows, appear at conferences, etc. Sometimes, the mere sense of mutual trust and like has lead to long-term partnerships, where I integrate their business in my business and get equity in their company in return.

Networking *can* open doors that were hitherto closed. I have gotten roles in movies because of my network, as well as great references in the financial sphere. But, ultimately, these occurrences would have been almost impossible to predict. You can end up spending a lot of time networking and see no results whatsoever, unless you're smart about it.

Also, people who are already extraordinarily successful tend to react like beautiful women who are approached by desperate single guys: they run away. You don't want to be the desperate single guy in this equation. Instead of pursuing celebrities in your industry, let the celebs come to you, once you've established yourself as an authority in your field.

The reason I lumped together networking – in a professional sense – and friendships in one sub chapter, is that they should essentially be perceived as one and the same thing. You won't make friends with everyone you connect with on LinkedIn or do business with, but if you treat all your connections as you would treat friends, you're off to a great start. It will automatically ensure a certain degree of conscientiousness in your interaction.

I recently conducted an interview with the CEO of a company with which I collaborate. As I was about to edit and publish the interview, I realized that I had pressed a wrong button by mistake, and switched off his audio feed. Annoying as it was, I treated the incident like I would have if the CEO were a friend of mine. I simply explained to him what had happened, apologized, and offered to redo the interview whenever was convenient for him. It was unfortunate, but there's really no way around owning up to your mistakes and treating them in an honorable manner.

The overarching point I want to make in this chapter is that networking and your social circle are aspects of the same thing. You don't want to network with people if their morals are dubious or incompatible with your values. The same thing goes for your friends. But instead of deleting all your non-entrepreneur friends from Facebook, I suggest that you simple see who sticks around, and who doesn't. If you keep adding to your network at a steady pace, some of the people you collaborate with will be the Bill Gates' of tomorrow. This is how you should look at it.

There is one final aspect that I need to address in this section. That has to do with the level of support you receive from your surroundings. As I recently shared on one of my YouTube channels, my ex-wife once told me that she hoped I'd never become famous. I didn't think much of the statement, when she said it, but in retrospect I have come to realize that it affected me immensely. Without even noticing, I stopped pursuing acting, and I truly believe this was a subconscious reaction to me knowing that she didn't support it. Also, when I remarried and moved to the US, I suddenly found myself surrounded by supportive and encouraging people. It hardly seems like a coincidence that this is when my business success started and accelerated.

Surround Yourself With Successful People, and You Will Have Success.

Verdict: true.

12. Trust No One

Once you start recruiting people, you will quickly realize that many people – the vast majority, in fact – let you down. It's not that they steal your car, ridicule you in public, or empty your company account, but rather that *they make promises, and fail to deliver on them*. This type of behavior can be extremely dangerous for obvious reasons: their performance reflects back on you. Their failure to deliver may put you on the spot and result in you suddenly have to deal with the tasks they were assigned. Also, you may need to spend time on recruiting again. Finding trustworthy people has become a big priority for me these days, much more so than seemingly skillful people. Skills are worthless if the individual possessing them is incapable of adhering to deadlines.

Professor of Leadership Communications, Conor Neill, suggested that we use the following three criteria to evaluate whether people can be trusted (enough for us to hire or collaborate with them):

Trustworthy people:

1. Recognize their own errors.

2. Tell you what you don't want to hear.

3. Believe in you.

With that in mind, let me share with you a recent story from my own life.

Until recently, I collaborated with a bright young man, let's call him Edward, who had a flair for doing research and writing it down in a very systematic manner. I was quite thrilled when he contacted me and offered to volunteer as a researcher and co-writer of my monthly investment report. I looked at his previous work, and it was thorough and of high quality. Edward struck me as persistent and meticulous. I told him that, if he could deliver what I needed for one month, I'd be happy to put him on the payroll. We were both happy with that agreement.

After a week of great collaboration, he suddenly stopped answering my emails and messages. This caused some minor issues, since he had started curating various news item, on which I used to base my YouTube videos. When he failed to deliver, I had to curate content myself, which took time away from the tasks on which I was working. About three days later, I heard back from him, and he told me an odd story about how his laptop had been locked away in his sister's car, to which he didn't have access. I gave him the benefit of the doubt, but told him that, in the future, I would expect him to simply notify me if for some reason he couldn't deliver on time, since it made our workflow break down if he didn't. I interpreted his actions as immaturity, since he's in his mid 20s. He wrote me back that he totally understood, and that he would improve in the future.

Fast-forward another two weeks or so. Edward had delivered on time, so I asked him if he felt ready to write a section for my monthly investment newsletter, as we had initially discussed. Not only was he willing, but he clearly expressed that he would be honored to do so, and that he could have it ready by Wednesday the following week. Wednesday came, and around 10 pm I had received nothing from Edward, so I wrote and asked him if he was still on track. He replied immediately, that he was just wrapping up, and would send it before he went to bed. When I got up Thursday, there was still no email from Edward. I wrote him again, asking for an estimated time of delivery, and reminded him that it didn't have to be perfect, since I would edit it, and a third person would proofread it. Once again, he assured me that he would deliver later that day. I started to have my doubts, but since he had been working hard during the previous weeks, I once again gave him the benefit of the doubt. The report was due Saturday, on which date it would go out to 20,000 subscribers.

When Friday came, I wrote Edward once again, telling him that I would need the report immediately, or I would have to write it myself. I asked him to simply send me what he had, and I could then finish it. No answer. As you've probably guessed, I ended up writing the report myself.

As if to add some sprinkle to an already rather absurd cake, 13 days later, Edward wrote me a long message. I had not expected to ever hear from him again. He started with a brief apology, and then progressed into a series of suggestions as to how we could expand our collaboration in the future. He also stated that he would obviously need to get on the payroll, if he was to keep on working for me. I deliberately didn't respond. He kept writing new suggestions for how we could collaborate every day, and I found it highly interesting to observe what he wrote. It should be noted that all his suggestions were really great and would add great value to my business, as well as relieve me of significant workloads, if they were in fact implemented. I finally wrote him back and told him that I was happy to hear from him, but that for me, reliability is key. On this basis, I could not defend continuing our collaboration. I also told him that it wasn't personal, that I held no grudge against him, but that I had to look after my business first and foremost, and that I could not risk taking him on, considering his track record. A few days later, he wrote me back, telling me that he had never been fired before, and that it had given him the opportunity to do some soul-searching. He also wrote that he had realized he needed to work on his communication and emotional intelligence skills. I think he was hoping for me to reconsider, but I would've been a fool to do so.

Edward also wrote that he had started working for a marketing company that had some interesting opportunities for me, and asked if he could put me on their mailing list. I agreed to this, as long as I would not be collaborating with him directly. He replied that I would receive an email from them "later today". Three days later, he asked me if I had received the email. I told him I had not. He wrote me that I would receive it by the next morning. Four days later, he wrote me that I would receive the email Monday. I wrote him back:

"No worries. Just saying that there's no need to say that stuff will happen 'tomorrow' and then leave people hanging without updating them. I know it's normal practice, but it just reflects poorly on you and whomever you're working for. Again, not trying to lecture you or act like a jerk, just saying how it's perceived by many people".

Eleven days later, he wrote me a long message, explaining how it wasn't like him not to live up to responsibilities and many other things. He then produced a far-fetched excuse as to why we couldn't communicate in the future, since he had started working for a company with which I had previously collaborated. It made no sense at all, and I decided to stop answering.

I never received the email, by the way.

I'm sure Edward had no ill intentions, but he breached the

first of Conor Neill's rules when he told me the story about his sister's car and more or less blamed me for not having created a proper work schedule for him. He breached the second rule when he told me that he could easily deliver on time, since he simply told me what he thought I wanted to hear. He didn't need to breach the third rule, since one is all you need.

We normally tend to focus on people's motives and intentions. If the intentions are good, we are often lenient. This rule doesn't apply in business. You need reliable collaborators and employees, and if people don't have the skills you need them to have, or if they are incapable of delivering on time, you have to let them go, sooner rather than later.

In his classic "wealth-growing" book, *The Richest Man in Babylon*, George Samuel Clason writes of a poor man, who decides to invest his money with a brickmaker, who's looking to buy jewels and sell them with a profit. But alas, the cunning Phoenicians trick the brickmaker and sell him colored glass instead of jewels. One of the points of this story is that when you take advice, you should do so from experts only. This ties back in with what I just wrote about good intentions not being sufficient for you to trust others, at least not with your money or your business. People may have fine diplomas, but if they don't have basic collaboration skills, whatever specializations they may have are useless.

In sum: trust experts in various niches. Experts are experienced, open-minded, and reliable individuals. If they only have one of these qualities, however, they may not be trustworthy. People are usually very quick to show you whether they can be trusted or not. So instead of hiring someone full-time right away, or giving them a flat fee to complete a task, give them a small assignment first, see how they perform, provide them with feedback, and repeat. If your feedback is received well and if it's actually integrated in their future work, then you take on less of a risk hiring them later. Use Conor Neill's three criteria to determine whether you can trust people.

Trust No One.

Verdict: false, but…

13. Outsource Everything

Now that you know how to determine whether you can trust someone, you're ready to hire people.

But should you really outsource everything?

There is no simple answer to this question. My personal experience has been that it is very liberating to outsource work, but it is equally hard to find employees who are trustworthy *and* skillful.

Companies usually outsource work if they can save money on production and thus increase their profits. But as a startup entrepreneur this logic can rarely be applied. If you do so, you will quickly arrive at the conclusion that you can't outsource anything, since the costs of doing so will simply take away from you current measly profits.

All else equal, the only thing you can save by outsourcing at early stages is time. And that is exactly why you should consider outsourcing as early as possible. When you're still in the process of planning your empire, you will do the heavy lifting yourself, but even at this stage it can be helpful to recruit someone to do the most trivial tasks. Jobs such as market research, collecting various information, and outreach can just as easily be done by a remote assistant who works at a significantly lower hourly rate than people you could hire using traditional methods.

If those skills lie outside your main area of expertise, you can waste enormous amounts of time teaching yourself skills and subsequently doing the work. It's not a matter of whether you *can* do it yourself. The question is, whether you *should* do it yourself. I see it over and over again: "Oh, I can easily teach myself how to code, program, design websites, run Facebook ads," etc. Sure you can, but you will waste valuable time doing tasks that you can pay someone from an emerging economy do for $8/hour or less.

You're not being smart by doing it yourself; you're being ignorant and foolish. Don't forget the big picture. You're not just selling a product. You're not even running a company. You're planning how to build an empire. Would the emperor till the dirt around his palace, just because he wants to prove to himself that he's capable of doing it?

The real balancing act has to do with this: what are your core skills? Are you a web developer? Are you a copywriter? Do you possess a particular practical knowledge? Whatever you're an expert at, is what you should be doing. Anything beyond that, you should try to outsource. If you think it'll be too expensive, rethink your MVP. Could you settle for less in order to launch? These are important questions, since you can end up spending too much time solving tasks that others could have undertaken.

On a final note, I want to say this: if the nature of your business allows you to outsource most – or even all – tasks, you should consider doing so. I have found great (and horrible) employees on Upwork.com, who were experts in their fields, especially in copywriting, web design, and the types of tasks that may as well be done by someone else. Obviously, the purpose of outsourcing isn't to give you time to relax and watch Netflix, but to give you time to focus on the big picture, and work on the tasks that only you can complete.

I would always choose a $5,000 monthly profit with little or no effort over a $20,000 monthly profit working 80 hours a week. That time could be put to much better use. And since you've already built one successful, revenue generating business, chances are you are capable of building another one, which would be much more sustainable and profitable in the long run.

Outsource Everything.

Verdict: true, but...

14. Establish 7 Passive Income Streams

There is a widespread myth that millionaires on average have 7 income streams. If there is any base in this assertion, it may be rooted in the fact that most millionaires have several different *types* of income, e.g. dividends, interest, earnings, etc. It has nothing to do with running 7 different businesses, although many millionaires obviously run more than one business. Seven is not a magic number outside of folklore.

Using this as an end goal in and of itself makes little sense. I personally don't care whether my money comes from dividends, sales, or the money tree in my kitchen. The only thing to be said about this may be that various types of income can represent a diversification between multiple different asset classes, which is of course a smart thing to do *if you are already affluent*, but not necessarily something that should be your top priority as a budding entrepreneur. Clearly, it is smart to have several streams of income, but the basis of this idea is a misinterpretation of an observed phenomenon. The 7 income streams rule is – once again – based on the idea that:

If millionaires have it, that must be the reason they are millionaires. I will certainly become a millionaire if I do the same thing.

We might as well assume that:

Because millionaires have 4 cars on average, all you need is 4 cars, and you're guaranteed to become a millionaire.

Proponents of this idea don't understand the difference between causal relations and correlations. Millionaires have 4 cars *because* they are millionaires, not the other way around. Just as they have 7 types of income streams *because* they are millionaires.

This twisted logic may be the most widespread and downright harmful way of thinking, yet it spreads like wildfire. In rhetoric, it is also known as *an argument from ignorance*. Danish author and playwright, Ludvig Holberg, ridiculed this very way of thinking in his 1723 play, *Erasmus Montanus*, in which the protagonist returns to his peasantry parents and uses "logical deduction" to conclude that:

"Mother does not fly. Nor does the stone. Hence, mother is a stone."

People were amused by the display of this type of idiocy almost 300 years ago. Let's leave that hanging for one moment, shall we? Proponents of this idea fail to use the most common of common sense. Interestingly, the same people also like to propagate that "college is a waste of money".

All that said, you should embrace the idea of not just running one business, simply because: one business = one lottery ticket

Even though you have much higher odds of succeeding as an entrepreneur than you do of winning the actual lottery, chances are you'll need more than one lottery ticket. In fact, all you need is one winning ticket. But to increase your odds, you need to make sure not fall too much in love with any single idea. At the very least, keep an open mind (trait openness) when you stumble on new things that could solve a problem, improve on something, or provide value for people. Many things have the potential to be turned into a product, even though it may seem too intangible at first glance.

In sum: you will eventually have multiple income streams, but focus on one at a time, and forget about the number 7. It's not a magic number; it's simply a misinterpreted observation.

Establish 7 Passive Income Streams.

Verdict: false, but...

15. Focus on the Possible, not the Impossible

There are two ways in which this statement can be interpreted. It can be understood as a reminder of the mindset that you should embrace, a mindset where the entrepreneur focuses not on the obstacles, but rather on the solutions. This is very basic and good way of thinking. If you are in the habit of focusing on the negative, get in the habit of asking yourself, what could be done to make possible that which currently seems impossible? Force yourself to write down several answers to the question, regardless of how ridiculous they seem in the moment. This will help you to leave a stagnant, counterproductive mindset behind.

There is, however, a second way of interpreting the statement, one that urges a sense of realism in the entrepreneur. I wholeheartedly believe that any successful entrepreneur must not only be filled with self-confidence, but also must understand that what is currently unattainable, could potentially become attainable, if the right information and knowledge is found.

There are obviously limitations for the individual, such as their current skills, IQ, background, knowledge, financial situation, network, geography, gender, etc. There are also limitations as to how many different venues of success can be pursued at once. I am currently balancing running two YouTube channels, writing two books, publishing a monthly investment report, an acting career, a marriage, friendships, investments, researching, collaborating, advising, speaking at conferences, and launching a new business. Although I enjoy the high activity level, I am approaching my maximum threshold.

I have a rather inflated sense of my own capabilities. For me it is therefore a great piece of advice to focus on the possible, not the impossible. That is, understanding that even though I can accomplish many things, some things are not attainable for me, because I simply don't posses the potential to gain the necessary skills. In other cases, it may be theoretically possible, but since I would have to spend years acquiring specific skills, certifications, building networks, etc., I should consider carefully whether the amount of effort that would be needed is really something I'm willing to put into it.

For people who are less naturally inclined to an unreasonable dosage of self-confidence, this piece of advice may not be as useful. In this case, the quality and utility of the advice really depends on the individual. Some individuals may have been brought up to believe that they should only pursue 'realistic goals'. These people may benefit from having their eyes opened to the fact that they can in fact accomplish much more than the trivial. However, I have witnessed very horrible outcomes when well-meaning people give this type of advice, making others believe they can truly achieve *anything*. In the most tragic example of all, a young girl that I knew took her own life because she was led to believe that she could become whatever she wanted to become. When reality finally dawned on her, and she realized that the career she had planned would never work out, she ended her life. Her dreams were crushed to a degree that gave her no reason to carry on. I will never forget her or her story. Her demise may have been what made me realize that not all is possible for everyone. We can all achieve a lot: far more than most of us are lead to believe. But none of us can accomplish anything or everything.

People have often described me as delusional. They have claimed that my dreams were completely unrealistic and unattainable. Many of these dreams have now become reality, but I still can't rule out that the criticism may be partially true. The question remains, however, whether it would have been helpful for me to believe those voices that claimed I was punching above my weight. I doubt it very much. This may be the only area in life where I'm inclined to advocate just a little bit of delusional behavior and grandiose thinking. I generally consider myself a hardcore fact and truth-seeker, but if we know that a rock solid self-belief and an inflated sense of self-capabilities are far more likely to shoot us off in a favorable trajectory, we would be fools to ignore that. There seems to be an extremely fine line between enormous self-confidence and delusions of grandeur. The former is viral, whereas the latter is a clinical diagnosis. Spiritual capitalists must strive for the middle ground.

Focus on the Possible, not the Impossible.

Verdict: true.

16. Never Lose Money

Warren Buffet and Tony Robbins are both frequently quoted as having said these words.

In fact, Buffet and Robbins are probably the two most prominent proponents of the wealth building strategies of the past. Their advice are absolutely solid, but only if you are an employee working the corporate ladder and only plan on making extra money for your retirement on investments. For people following the traditional route to mediocrity, or for people who are looking for a small amount of interest whilst preserving their wealth, this *is* golden advice.

However, when you're looking to build an empire, their advice is downright terrible. Tony Robbins in particular tends to quote the wisdom presented in the 1926 book, *The Richest Man in Babylon*, as well as Napoleon Hill's *Think and Grow Rich*. "Never lose money" is only a meaningful mantra if you're not in the business of taking calculated risks. If your most risky decision is to decide which blue chip stock to invest in, this mantra makes sense. But for the spiritual capitalist, it is merely noise. Name me one billion dollar investment, that wasn't considered risky at some point in time.

The reason it's such terrible advice to give to entrepreneurs is that, even though you don't necessarily need a lot of money to start a business, you cannot carry this scarcity mindset with you into running a successful business. You will need to pay for many services, e.g. web hosting, labor, analytics tools, subscriptions, books, courses, etc. None of these are particularly expensive, but if you invest your measly savings in stocks to see a 2-5% annual gain, your growth potential will diminish. You can turn to stocks later. But right now? You need to make your first couple of millions. Robbins and Buffet neglect to mention that.

Example: I used to spend hours looking for cheap books online. Not just any books, but specific books that I knew I needed to read to gain specific knowledge on a specific subject matter. Sometimes I would be unable to find the book I wanted for free. More often than not, I ended up not reading the book at all, or I would buy a used paperback version, that took weeks – sometimes months – to arrive, all just to save a few dollars. Back then, I didn't consider that if I spent, let's say, one hour finding a paperback that ultimately saved me $4, I would essentially pay myself $4 for one hour's work. I would've never taken a regular job at this rate, but out of sheer ignorance I was happy to "save money" using this method times over.

Never lose money has no deeper meaning beyond its immediate, intuitive message. Once you've made a fortune on your empire, then you can start taking advice from guys like Buffet and Robbins, but at the early stages of your life as spiritual capitalist, you'll do best to ignore them.

Never Lose Money.

Verdict: false.

17. Don't be in it for the Money

There's a widespread idea that entrepreneurs don't really care about making money, but are rather driven by passion. The truth is that one doesn't rule out the other. Most billionaires are passionate, and why wouldn't they be? The world is their oyster. But once again, we cannot conclude that a random characteristic of successful people is what made them successful. I do believe that passion, drive, willpower, self-motivation, or whatever you want to call it, is very important, but to claim that successful entrepreneurs are only in it for their vision of a better world is preposterous. That's the tale they're telling you, when they're interviewed on Fox Business, but it is, nonetheless, a tale. It's part of their brand.

In fact, this assertion is so naive that I can hardly perceive it as little other than establishment propaganda intended to keep people in their right place: mediocrity. I'm not writing this book expecting to make money from it, but that doesn't mean that I'm not interested in making money. Quite the contrary. I'm passionate about it, and the words are flowing out and down on the paper, but I am also doing it as part of my brand strategy. I want people to read the book and think:

"That Asger guy, he's on to something. I wish I read that book earlier."

I love to help people and open their eyes to a bigger world with more opportunities. But rest assured that my mission with this book is twofold: helping people *and* building my brand as an expert who likes to help people. And the latter will increase my value, and perhaps earn me more money in the long run. Inspiring and profiting are both my priorities, not just one of them.

Do some wealthy people become philanthropists?

Of course they do.

Are many entrepreneurs passionate about what they're doing?

Of course they are.

Do most entrepreneurs talk passionately about their business in an effort to build a brand as "one of the good guys"?

Absolutely.

The idea that successful people aren't in it for the money (which happens to be the name of one of my YouTube channels) is unnervingly naive. No public person wants you to think that they are primarily in it for the money, simply because it's bad for business. They don't want to be labeled as greedy.

While I understand and appreciate the rationale behind this piece of advice, there is something fundamentally wrong with that way of thinking, because it entails people lying to themselves and the entire world. I consider that intrinsically bad.

You should be focusing on the money from day one. In fact, you should be focusing on the money *before* day one. At times, you need to forget about the money, since it is true that you can't always just focus on how to get a few more bucks in. That kills your authenticity and it's shortsighted. You can have the best idea in the world, but if you can't sell it – in any way, shape or form – it won't make a viable business. So why would you want to start a business, without focusing on the money? Actually, if you did so, your business would fail miserably, which transforms the real meaning of this advice to:

Don't start a business.

Think about that the next time you hear a mainstream media financial guru saying this on TV.

My ideas never start with the money. But as soon as I know what I'm trying to build, I do some rough calculations and projections of expenses and income. If my most conservative estimates are feasible, I move on to a calculation of more positive scenarios. If they indicate that there could be a gold mine hidden here, I move on with the idea, until other things convince me to drop it, or until it's been set in motion.

My advice: do set out to become wealthy. But understand that it may take a long time. If you can add a flare of ideology to your business, more power to you. But don't fool yourself. Your motivation for doing extraordinary things is rooted in material or – at the very least – narcissistic aspirations.

Don't be in it for the Money.

Verdict: false.

18. Find a Niche Without Competition

Before the Internet, I would have approximately as many ideas as I do now. The main difference between now and then is that I used to think all my ideas were novel and that no one else had ever thought of them before. These days, I understand that even though I consider myself a highly creative, imaginative, and resourceful individual, only a small percentage of my ideas are actually novel. And I expect even the ones that are to pop up on Google in no more than a few years or months.

Humans in the twenty-first century all think they are unique and special, and to many people it's almost incomprehensible that an idea that occurred to them in the shower yesterday is also shared by tens of thousands of other individuals. The Internet may have reinforced this tendency. After all, we all watch the same shows, read the same articles, use the same social media, governed by the same algorithms. Inspiration doesn't just arise out of thin air; the things we hear, see, and read fuel it. It is therefore no great mystery that very few ideas are truly unique. In fact, creativity can be described as the phenomenon of pairing things that don't usually belong together. If you disagree, feel free to provide a better definition.

If you took two lab rats and subjected them to the same stimuli, would you wonder why they subsequently reacted in a similar manner? Would you ask yourself, "How come they aren't behaving in unique different ways?" They are, after all, unique individuals too. Although we are not lab rats, and although we are vastly more complex and complicated beings than rats, we don't like to think of ourselves as animals. But that doesn't change the fact that, if we're running on autopilot, so to speak, nature takes over, and we will do what the alpha elders of the tribe expects us to. Once again, this path leads to mediocrity.

This is yet another important reminder of the significance of human nature. We are all different, but on a very fundamental level, we are the same. We react, feel, think, and associate in ways that are almost identical. We can't change the fundamental structure of our brains, and it takes ages to change our personalities. How we *act* may be the only potential difference, and where we can make an impact. Looking back at my life, I've always simply acted on an idea, the minute I felt it was worth pursuing. In most cases, I ended up realizing how time-consuming, or unprofitable, it would be, and I dropped it again. But over the past five years or so, I have come to learn that this skill, decisiveness, is actually quite rare in humans. When you pair it with discipline, knowledge, and strategy, you have a powerful potion.

How is this related to niche markets? Well, if you experience some sort of frustration, see something that could be improved, or that no one has yet developed; chances are that others think and feel the same way. This is a good thing, since it makes it feasible that there is a need and a market for your product or service, but it's bad, because chances are that others have already moved on the same impulse.

Taking on the biggest mainstream market is probably not the smartest decision. But, then again, if you have your own take on it – if you can do it better, cheaper, easier, more entertaining, or better branded – why not? Your persistence is what will drive you to win, not finding some little niche that can earn you a few hundred bucks each month. Remember, you don't just want to replace your corporate job with a similar job that you've created.

In that case, the only difference would be that you don't have a boss, coworkers, or anyone to tell you what to do next and keep you accountable, and no security whatsoever. Niche businesses can be profitable, but not all niche businesses are, so you must choose carefully.

Also, there are plenty of niches, but you'll struggle to find one without competition. Niche businesses may work better if you're selling a relatively low volume of high revenue products. However, if you're selling cheap products with a low profit per item, making a niche business profitable can be extremely challenging.

Find a Niche Without Competition.

Verdict: false.

19. Follow your Heart

"Follow your heart" must be one of the most pervasive and persistent pieces of advice given by people from all walks of life, to people from all walks of life. One of the reasons I'm not a huge fan of this advice is that, although I'm passionate about many things, I know that not everybody feels like that. I've heard countless people express that they don't have a passion. Similarly, others have many passions.

I'm passionate about many things. A few examples: playing the piano, having sex, eating chocolate, and seeing friends. Those are some of my favorite things. So should I turn them into businesses? I don't really see how. I also love acting, but I'm doing that in between all the other things I do. I don't plan on realizing all my dreams (following all my heart's desires, if you will) through acting. On the contrary, in fact. I'm contemplating moving into movie production in the future, something that success in *other areas* will help me do. I am interested in cryptocurrencies, for instance, which is where my main income comes from at the moment. But do I have a deep, insatiable desire to think about cryptocurrency all the time, every day? No. I'd much rather play the piano, have sex, act, and see my closest friends (separately, that is).

As the old Danish proverb goes: "No arms, no cookies."

Apart from being cruel, there's also a fundamental truth

hidden here: the thing you make a career out of must be something you're good at, but it must also be something that you can realistically monetize in some way, shape or form. If you have no arms, you simply won't be helping yourself to any cookies from the top shelf.

Yet many "experts" keep repeating that if you do what you love, money will follow. I think money follows, if you love what you do (and if it's a thing that can be profited from). This is not at all the same thing as doing what you love. You can find love in many things. Appreciate what you're working on, whatever it is. That's a much better advice in my opinion.

Businesswoman, Penelope Trunk, wrote on this topic:

"It's preposterous that we need to get paid to do what we love because we do that stuff anyway. None of us loves just one thing. [...] Do not what you love; do what you are."

Thankfully, Mark Cuban also seems to agree with me:

"I hear it all the time. 'I'm not going to quit, it's my passion.' Or I hear it as advice to students and others: 'Follow your passion.' What a bunch of BS. 'Follow your passion' is easily the worst advice you could ever give or get."

Personally, I have many dreams that I aspire to realize in the future. But those dreams are so big that my odds of realizing them right here and now would be extremely low. That doesn't mean that I don't keep them in the back of my mind, and it also doesn't mean that I don't have a plan for how to realize them. I do. But part of that plan is to focus on other matters for the time being, until I'm in a place where I can easily bring them into fruition. I'm growing arms, so I can have the top shelf cookies later. That's why I choose to do what I do, and simply enjoy the ride. I'm building my empire now, and I enjoy building it. It is hard work, but it's very satisfactory. Once my empire has reached a certain size, I'll have different options and opportunities.

There are many other varieties of "follow your heart", by the way. A few examples: "Trust in the universe", "Don't do it if doesn't feel right", and my all time favorites, "do what you're meant to do", and "find your life purpose".

All of these are more or less verbatim quotes by Oprah Winfrey. There's something very powerful about a women with Oprah's background, struggles, status, and success, stating these mantras. Unfortunately, just like in the case of Tony Robbins, they're all hollow clichés with no deeper meaning, and they will only help you become more stuck in a mediocre mindset. All the statements presuppose the existence of higher powers and, regardless of your personal beliefs, I'm sure we can agree that praying for wealth and success doesn't make you wealthy or successful. In fact, there's something very dangerous about thinking of success as something God-given, since that implies that it's essentially out of your control. You're not going to sit around and wait for your success. True spiritual capitalists seize the day and take deliberate, planned, strategically smart and calculated steps towards their long-term goals. Every single day.

Oprah also talks about "the work you're meant to do". I want to be absolutely clear: you are not meant to do any specific work. But when you're successfully pursuing what you want, it often times feels as if it's the case. This line of thinking, however, is not only ignorant, it is also judgmental and dangerous, possibly leading people to "seek their purpose" without ever finding it. It must also lead some people to wonder why God thinks they're made to sit behind counters and desks at minimum wage.

Hint: it's not there.

Don't listen to Oprah for entrepreneurial advice. For some reason, many people who experience extreme success tend to start talking about this kind of thing, as I described earlier. I really think it's an expression of narcissism. When we experience success, it's easy to get carried away and think:

"God has a higher purpose for me. I'm chosen to do this. It wasn't a coincidence."

But think about it. If God selected Oprah to "do what she's meant to do", what does God think that *you* are meant to do? Or your parents? Or grandparents? Did he also give them what they deserved? And if so, what does that tell us about Oprah? This is narcissism of the worst kind, where the narcissist doesn't even see what's going on and all of a sudden feels so entitled, that it must be God himself who has granted them the honor of having this slice of success. The irony is that Oprah has worked so hard, that she truly deserves every bit of her success. But for some reason, that just seems too implausible for her to embrace, and the heavenly father must be introduced to justify the authority she has managed to claim.

Finally, returning to Earth, you cannot expect to always do what feels good. You'll work many late nights, make many hard decisions, face many defeats, hire and fire, and it's not going to be a walk in the park. If you perceive any of these things as "signs" that you're treading the wrong path, you might as well just quit now. Having an overarching vision will motivate you through the tough times, as well as remind you that you will indeed arrive at a place where what you're doing feels great. But right now, it's time to sacrifice, and sacrifice by definition doesn't feel good.

Follow your Heart.

Verdict: false.

20. Habits are Key to Success

Habits can be defined as follows:

fixed ways of thinking, acting or feeling, acquired through repetition of actions or experiences.

A lot has been written and said about the importance of habits. Possessing the theoretical knowledge about something is not enough to succeed since knowledge is no guarantee of execution. Also, most things are accomplished through persistence and repetition. Habits, as opposed to knowledge are, per definition, persistent. If we have counter-productive habits, we will be inefficient. If we have productive habits, we will be industrious.

We could say that habits are a sort of self-instilled mental autopilot. It is therefore essential that our autopilot isn't set on a course that leads to our demise. The idea that habits are crucial is not only supported by psychological science, it has been more or less common knowledge since ancient times.

Aristotle wrote:

"We are what we repeatedly do. Excellence is not an act, but a habit."

I am a huge fan of habits. The best part about habits is that due to the plastic (flexible) nature of the human brain, we can actually rewire ourselves with new habits, simply by repeating – and thus reinforcing – new actions for a period of time. A person's habits may actually tell us more about them than their actions.

I must attribute a large part of my own success to new habits that I've managed to reinforce, until they became so stable, that they are now an integral part of my modus operandi. In most cases, I have done this by implementing one simple, self-enforced rule.

I have only one point of criticism of the line of thinking represented by the Aristotle quote. The average human being is unquestionably a result of their habits. But there are a few qualities that most successful people possess, that are not readily encompassed or explained by habits. Specifically, I'm thinking about flexibility. Most habits are healthy because of the circumstances in which they occur.

However, when extraordinary situations arise, habits that are normally productive can be downright detrimental for success. On a corporate level, the most obvious example might be the DVD and VHS rental giant, Blockbuster. It failed to adapt to changing times with new demands, but simply kept doing what they "knew to be successful".

On a more individual level, let's say you have your entire day filled out with productive habits. But if your virtual assistant quits, your spouse wants a divorce, your customer database is hacked, or your product warehouse burns to the ground, these habits will not help you. Similarly, if you're currently answering emails, because you established the habit of doing so every day between noon and 1 o'clock, and you suddenly get a creative impulse that might lead to a new business, then you'd be foolish not to write it down.

In fact, when this happens to me, I've made a habit out of simply creating a new document and writing down the idea as fast as I possibly can. I then return to the task I was working on. At the end of the day, I archive the new business idea in a document dedicated for that, and elaborate on it, if I'm inspired to do so. Once or twice a month, I look at all the documents and folders where I wrote down my ideas. When a little time has passed, it's typically easy to throw away maybe half of them right away. The other half, however, I expand on. I then present them to a friend for feedback. If an idea makes it through these stages, I may just push the button and move on with it.

In sum: if we don't consciously design the habits that constitute our every day life, our habits will consist of that which is most convenient or "feels best" in the moment. Our animal nature will govern our actions. To become highly productive, or *high-performers*, as many people call it, we must carefully plan and build habits that will help us reach our long-term goals. The habits that you will benefit from may not be the same ones from which Bill Gates benefits most. Creating our own habits, however, is crucial. Not only does this give us a tremendous competitive advantage, since most people don't design habits of their own choosing, but it also enables us to make far more of our time, which is really what all growth-hacking is about. In the end, we all have the same 24 hours available each day. As spiritual capitalists, we simply cannot waste most of them on performing random activities. Even if you're sitting for 10 hours a day in your office, you should ask yourself how many effective work hours you are having on an average day. Whatever the answer is, many small habits can be implemented to increase your efficiency. For instance, given that most humans are at their optimum during the first couple hours after they get up, that's when you should do your most mentally demanding tasks. More trivial tasks that don't demand as much cognitive function should be allocated for later in the day. Many books have been written about this, but I think it's hard to make a specific formula that works for everyone. Also, implementing new habits sounds easy, but it's not. Far from it, in fact. In the last chapter of this book, I provide a tangible method to get you started.

Habits are Key to Success.

Verdict: true.

21. People Sabotage Themselves Because They Secretly Fear Success

According to Tony Robbins, self-sabotage is the biggest reason people fail to achieve their financial goals. Robbins believes that, on some level, people think that having lots of money will bring them more unhappiness than happiness, so they tend to focus on the negative aspects of wealth.

Once again, I must declare my utter discontent with this nonsense. If people knew what it really meant to be wealthy, they might have such concerns. But the reality is, almost all people dream of being filthy rich. While it's true that there are certain cultural taboos around money, people certainly aren't afraid of either money or success. They desire it. Typically, they haven't pondered deeply on the consequences of actually having it. As I see it, Robbins once again uses a made-up claim to create the illusion that you can easily become the best version of yourself. All you need to do is *find your passion* and *stop sabotaging yourself*.

All that said, many people *are* afraid of "putting themselves out there". Their main way of "sabotaging themselves", however, is almost always by *never beginning* in the first place. Taking the decision to start is by far the biggest hurdle you must pass, and those who are capable of that usually don't hinder their own success. This is yet another nonsense myth that may occur in some tiny fraction of a fraction of the population. But it has no merit in reality and, therefore, no relevance whatsoever for hardly anyone.

As long as you're aware of the dangers of perfectionism that I talked about previously, you will likely not have any problems with early self-sabotage because you're afraid of success.

Robert Kiyosaki, author of the bestselling book, *Rich Dad Poor Dad*, wrote what may be the only relevant thing about fear and success. According to Kiyosaki, people with a "poor mindset" are being held back by self-doubt. These people typically wait for luck and opportunity to come their way, whereas the rich create their own opportunities out of obstacles. On this basis, Kiyosaki concludes that it is rather the bold people, not the smart, who ultimately succeed.

I wholeheartedly agree with this, but it should be noted that, while this may be characteristic for the average person, it doesn't apply to most spiritual capitalists. Therefore, it may not be relevant to you, since you've already made the decision to rise above the average. The most use we can make of this fact may be that it gives us an improved understanding of how others think, which can be helpful, since the average person may very well constitute the majority of your customer base. All that said, self-confidence is crucial for success in business, as is the ability to demonstrate it.

Do most people have dreams? Sure.

Are most people afraid of the uncertainties associated with the pursuit of their dreams? Sure.

Are they really sabotaging themselves, because they don't want to be rich and unhappy? I doubt it very much.

People Sabotage Themselves Because They Secretly Fear Success.

Verdict: false.

CHAPTER 3
THE DOCTRINES OF SPIRITUAL CAPITALISM

Even the most hardcore rational and scientifically-minded individuals need to embrace certain spiritual elements in order to truly rise to power. Similarly, people who are very focused on spirituality need to realize that they must embrace scientific observations in order to increase their odds for success in any given situation. If following our intuition means that we always do what is least likely to pay off – in a statistical sense – there's almost no chance that we'll succeed. But, more importantly, there's zero chance for success unless you create things and put them out in the real world.

The doctrines of spiritual capitalism are the basics for extreme success. They can be applied by anyone who's at the early stages of rising to power. Although they do not comprise a fully detailed practical guide, they offer you the basic framework – a template if you will – that you can fill in with the specifics that apply to your life. If you follow the doctrines, you will optimize your odds for extreme success. You can fail in so many ways, but if you follow the doctrines religiously, you will still succeed. If may sound overly optimistic, but it's not. Keep in mind that the doctrines *are* listed in chronological order, meaning that the first doctrine overrules the second one. Both are important, but not equally important.

1st Doctrine:
Work for Yourself, Now

Thus far, you have worked for other people. Starting right now, you will work for yourself, every single day. You will start executing.

This may sound banal. Let me elaborate. If you have plans to open a company, you are essentially doing nothing. If you take notes every once in a while, or if you've been thinking about some brilliant business ideas over the past few years, you've done nothing. You are not one step closer to success than you were back when you started thinking. If you had been executing since the first time that idea came to mind, you would've come far already. But you didn't, and that's why you've accomplished absolutely nothing.

It's not about having a goddamn idea; it's about executing it! Again, let me reiterate and elaborate. As I stated in the beginning of this book, you can have the best idea in the world, but if it stays in your drawer – or your mind – nothing will come of it. It doesn't make you a genius. I used to think myself a sage, because I had so many ideas, but I eventually realized that I was a fool for not executing any of them. Others have likely had the same idea, and they didn't execute it either. No idea is great in and of itself. Unless you put it out in the world, it doesn't exist. I cannot count the number of times people have refused to tell me about some billion dollar idea, because they were scared that I – or someone else – would steal it. I've had ideas stolen from me in the past, and I'm not the least bit mad about it. Truth be told, I would've never ever executed any of those ideas, so I only have respect for the people who managed to do so, even though it was my idea.

The trophy isn't awarded to the person who came up with it first. The trophy is awarded to whoever manages to execute the idea. If you truly understand what this means, you also understand that you need to start working on *your* empire right this very moment. If you're not actively working on your own success, you will never have success. This is not an assumption; it's a fact.

A couple years ago, a friend of mine asked for some help regarding his thesis. It was 200 pages long, but only supposed to be 100. He had less than a week to cut it in half, without ruining it. I helped him with that, and a few months later, after he'd graduated with flying colors, we were on the phone again. At the time I was writing a different book, and he asked me how it was coming along. I told him I was approaching 400 pages. He said:

"I simply don't understand how you do it. How can you write so many pages?"

I immediately asked him, what he meant. After all, he had just written a golden 200 pages master thesis! He replied:

"Yeah, but that's different. I had to."

That's when I had the epiphany. What my friend said was essentially that he *felt* like he had to, because other people expected him to do so. He had no choice.

And that's how almost all people lead their lives: they get up hours before they are rested, because that's what others expect of them. They go to work, because that's what others expect of them. They live their entire life on the basis of other people's expectations. This is, of course, a little more complex than I've portrayed it here, but the main point is that it's an integral part of societal structure that we make agreements with others – whether they be employers, partners, children, family, or friends – that we will do such and such, and in return, they give us something back.

Answer this question: why do you work for others, year after year, but never for yourself?

Have you ever even considered the absurdity in this?

If you don't take control of this mechanism, you will live the life that others expect of you. And then it's over. And, rest assured, that these others do not expect you to become a multi-millionaire. All they will do is help you maintain the status quo. I should stress, that this is not a critique of the powers that be, the way society works, or people in general. I'm not saying that you're "being used" by anyone. This is merely an observation of how things function. We all do what we have to. But, for some reason, that translates into: *we do what we have to, in order to maintain relations with others that we depend on.*

The day I fully understood this, was the day I changed my life and started working for myself. I kept my job, since I needed it to cover my expenses, but I implemented one simple rule, that led to enormous change. Each morning when I woke up, I would spend at least two hours working for myself. That is, working on something that could bring me great success in the long-term. Back then, that was writing a fiction novel. Initially, it felt strange. My day job was doing translations for TV, so I already worked from home, and each day I would wake up to a deadline, typically around 10 pm. The seemingly logical thing to do was to get started, so I wouldn't risk not making my deadline. But if I did that, I would work 6-7 hours straight, and my cognitive resources would then be so depleted, that I could hardly think, let alone find the energy to write my novel. The mechanism had kept me in a counter-productive spiral for years.

After having followed this rule for a month or so, I found that my mindset shifted. Previously, I had put a lot of energy and focus into the translations I did. When people asked me what I did, I would reply that I worked for a translation company. But now the translation work was really just something I did on the side, at least mentally. Not that I scaled back my hours with the translation company – I typically worked around 50 hours per week – but I simply changed my mental priorities, and I started working just as much on the novel, and later on my new business. When I woke up, I would think about the novel and my new business. I would sit right down and work on it, and only when I couldn't postpone my translation assignment any longer, would I start working on it, so I didn't miss the deadline. After having done this for about 6 months, my business generated enough profit that I could resign from the translation job.

Let me break it down to its devastating simplicity.

It's not about *finding* motivation. It's about understanding that if you want success, you have *no other choice* than executing right now. Not working for yourself every single day equals failure. Period.

If you don't try, you have already failed. Having a dream, or even a plan, is dreaming and planning, which is not the same as trying.

Your failure is *guaranteed*, if you don't start executing right now.

And as you read this, you probably think something to the effect of:

"But I need time to dedicate myself to my business idea. I'm too busy right now. I'm working towards freeing up more time, so I can dedicate myself fully to my dream, but right now, it's just impossible."

That's the mistake everyone – except the wildly successful – makes.

It's an error of judgment. Your priorities are wrong.

What, exactly, do you mean when you say that you're working on freeing up more time?

It's not about having more time; it's about fully committing on a mental level.

It's about waking up and focusing on your empire. You have to go to work? Well, if you have to, you have to, but look at your job as a minor inconvenience that takes up some of your time.

You don't have any time?

Yes, you do.

I understand that most people have jobs, partners, and kids, and that all those take away time. But honestly, if you have time to read or listen to this book, you have spare time. If you get up at 6 am, you could get up at 5 am. If you unwind on weekends, you have plenty of available time.

If you want success, you must put in the hours. You have to do so right now.

Again, think of it this way: you have big dreams, and you've had them for years.

Why haven't they been realized yet?

Because you haven't done anything to make them happen.

If you don't start executing and working for yourself, your failure is 100% guaranteed.

It is painstakingly simple, but I know only a few people who really truly embrace this realization. And that's another key aspect; it's not about having an intellectual understanding that you should put in more hours for yourself, work more structured, etc. It's about having a downright epiphany, where you truly fully understand that, if you don't *do it*, it will never happen. There is no tomorrow in the realm of spiritual capitalism.

Understand that, from now on, everything is about you growing as a person and as a business. When you wake up, that's what you think about. When you go to bed, that's what you think about. You already have a job? Get over it. Do your job with minimal effort and focus on working for yourself and on yourself. You're obviously not going to be a world famous CEO from one day to the next, so you need to adjust your expectations accordingly. Vision is easy; execution is hard.

As I mentioned, I've run multiple companies in the past. But it wasn't until I had this realization that I started being successful. And again, this is not some piece of advice that you can agree or disagree with. It's indisputable fact that none of your dreams will come true unless you start executing right now. It is gospel. And it's the essence of spiritual capitalism.

Without this realization you are guaranteed to achieve nothing.

2nd Doctrine:
Make and Follow the Rules

The second doctrine has to do with the implementation of the first, but it also serves as a framework for working efficiently and effectively. I already talked about habits of successful people in the second chapter, and from that discussion, it should be clear that habits are important. But as per its definition, a habit takes time to form and maintain. It can take years for habits to become truly ingrained in us, and there's also the risk that a habit that once brought us success, turns into an obstacle. That is why you must make and follow your own rules. Rules are related to habits, but in many ways they are better, because we are already "in the habit of following rules".

There are countless things you could do right now to grow, plan, and nurture your empire. You could probably easily create a to do list with hundreds of tasks. Humans have an innate tendency to always attack the nearest enemy. Evolution has ensured that we always try to rid ourselves of those threats or obstacles that are in our closest vicinity. But remember that success is gained by implementing a series of counter intuitive measures. I could easily fill each and every day in my life with tasks that need to be solved immediately. None of those tasks, however, would bring me a single step closer to my long-term goals, which is why I need to change my priorities and implement rules. All rules should be oriented directly towards your long-term goals.

You already know that you can no longer follow other people's rules. That does not mean that you won't be following any rules. In fact, you'll be following more rules than ever, but they will all be rules that you make for yourself.

Human beings are weak. In any given scenario, we seek the solution that is easiest to deal with emotionally. You're not an emotional person? What we're talking about here runs much deeper than your unique personality. It is something that applies to all of us. What is considered emotionally comfortable may differ from person to person, but we all have an emotional autopilot and subconscious processes guide most of its actions. Granted, some people may have an easier time doing what is emotionally uncomfortable for most others, but not a single human being is born for success. Survival and procreation is what we're hardwired for, not extreme success.

To persevere, you must do the counter intuitive and you must do it over and over again. Spending all your mental energy on success is inherently a counter intuitive endeavor. It's a major struggle, even for the most disciplined individuals. That's why we can't rely on discipline, and that's also where the second doctrine of spiritual capitalism comes in.

Even though you've fully grasped the first doctrine, you cannot rely on yourself to work consistently towards your long-term goals on any regular basis. You have to make your own rules, and you have to follow them religiously.

Breaking rules that you set up for yourself is much worse than breaking rules that others impose on you. Think about the times you showed up late for work or completed an assignment all wrong. You felt embarrassed and fearful for your livelihood. What actually happened is that you cost some company owner a few dollars in lost work hours. It's no big deal. But when you break your own rules, you are essentially screwing yourself over. You made a promise to the one person who should be dearest to you, and you broke it. You're letting yourself down. You have to understand that rules aren't intrinsically bad; they only feel bad because we are accustomed to them being made by others.

What Rules?

How many times have you actually taken action after having read a brilliant book on entrepreneurship?

One of the reasons it's hard to put theory into practice is that you simply don't know where to start. Right now, for instance, you might be wondering what sorts of rules you should consider creating and implementing in your life.

Let me provide you with a simple system, that will not only illuminate how to get started making rules, but that will also make it obvious how little you're currently doing to achieve success, hence motivating you.

Write a list of (a) all the things you have to do, (b) all the things you do, and (c) all the things you want to do. This list will inevitably be an odd mix of practical matters, work obligations, social encounters, and big lofty goals.

When I started out, mine looked something like this:

ACTIVITY	DESCRIPTION
Work	Day job.
Novel	Main ambition.

Health	Going to the gym or jogging.
App	An early stage tech company.
Acting	Going to auditions, rehearsing, etc.
Studying	A masters program I was enrolled in.

Go on. Write down your list as it currently looks. Remember to include all activities that you perform on a weekly basis.

Now that you have a list with all your priorities, every day, start writing down how long you spend on each activity. Create a document dedicated to it, or use a notebook. If you're on-the-go, make notes on your phone, and transfer them to your main document, once you get home. Break everything down in 15-minute intervals.

My first week schedule looked something like this:

DAY	ACTIVITY	# HOURS	TOTAL HOURS	TOTAL %
Monday	Work	6.5		
	Novel	0.25		
	Health	1.5		
Tuesday	Work	9.0		
	Studying	3.0		
	Acting	0.5		
Wednesday	Work	5.5		
	Health	1.5		

	App	1.0		
Thursday	Studying	5.0		
	App	1.0		
Friday	Work	4.5		
	Health	1.75		
Saturday	Novel	2.0		
Sunday	Novel	0.5		
	Health	1.5		
	Studying	5.0		
Week Total	Work		25.5	51%
	Studying		13.0	26%
	Health		6.25	12.5%
	Novel		2.75	5.5%
	App		2.0	4%
	Acting		0.5	1%

Let's use this overview to go over all the things that were wrong with this week. First of all, I had only worked 50 hours the entire week. I used to consider that impressive, but these days anything below 70 hours is a joke to me. Remember, I wanted to be an author, an actor, and an entrepreneur, yet I had spent more than twice as much time working out than I did working on my book. I had only spent 4% of my time working on the app, and a measly 1% of my time on acting. Looking at the table, I realized that I couldn't possibly call myself an author, let alone an actor or entrepreneur. I was an embarrassment to myself. The numbers had spoken their clear language, and they told me that I was first and foremost a worker bee.

But I didn't want to be a worker bee. I looked at the numbers again and identified some obvious places where I could make adjustments. Sunday, I had only worked 2 hours. If I had spent the entire day working on my novel, I would've spent more than 20% of my time writing. I also couldn't wrap my mind around the fact that I had spent 12.5% of my time in the gym. I was looking to get chiseled, sure, but other than my narcissism, I had no real purpose to visiting the gym.

I used the time-measurement system for almost three years before I didn't need it anymore. There are many lessons to be learned from it, the most important one being what you actually spend your time on.

As I mentioned earlier, the first rule I implemented was *start each day working at least two hours on the novel*. The novel was not only a lottery ticket, I had dreamed about publishing a novel for over a decade. It was also something that could be finished, as opposed to acting or working out, so it seemed logical to focus on that, until it was done.

As time passed, I collected much more data, and I continually adjusted my work efforts, so the discrepancy between what I wanted and what I did, became increasingly smaller. Implementing adjustments, however, must be done by making rules.

Here are examples of rules I've followed:

X. Start each day with coffee and reading for 30 minutes.

X. No matter how much I work for others, I must work more for myself.

X. Do at least 100 push-ups each day.

X. Work 12 hours each day, split into 2-hour blocks.

X. Work 16 hours a day, 6 days a week. Relax on the last day (the God complex model).

X. Spend 15 minutes each day answering emails and messages.

X. Dedicate 1 hour each day to complete things from my to do list.

One phenomenon that I've seen over and over again is people who decide to implement rules, but implement too many at a time. They essentially go from having an unstructured life, to following 12 rules the next day. These people always fail. And I mean *always*. Never implement more than one rule at a time, and remember that, although creating and following rules is extremely important, it's not as important as the first doctrine. If you truly realize that you must work for yourself each day, starting now, then you're golden. And if you consistently write down how you spend your time, you will be forced to make a decision: is this the life you want, where you spend 95% of your time working for others? Or are you willing to do what it takes and make the sacrifice? Are the goals you're working on in your spare time really your most important goals? How many hours do *you* spend in the gym each week?

There's no golden standard for the balance between working for others (while you still have to), and working for yourself, but you will obviously not accomplish anything extraordinary if, for example, you work on a new business 5 hours a week. That being said, working 5 hours for yourself each week is infinitely more than not working for yourself at all. But be realistic about it. If you punch in 5 hours per week, it'll take you 2 months to reach 40 hours, which you're happy to put in every week when working for others. Don't get comfortable. It's excruciating to work 80+ hours per week, but there are no natural laws that dictate that you can't or shouldn't. Just because we've had it easier than any generation before us in the history of humankind, doesn't mean that it's natural to work 40 hours each week and then unwind on the couch. Get over your entitlement complex. You want to be an emperor? Well, you weren't born in the palace, so you need to create your empire from scratch. I've worked 17-hour days for months back-to-back. That's almost three full-time position's worth of work hours. If I can do that, surely you can fit in an extra 40 hours working for you, even if you keep your corporate job.

Time is the only resource all humans have in more or less the same quantity, and all of this is related to how you spend your time. It's easy to work hard. Many people do it, but almost none of them are wealthy. Where the purpose of the first doctrine is to get you started, the purpose of the second doctrine is to force you to be effective without having to read dozens of growth-hacking books. When you make rules for your yourself, and survey how much time you spend on various tasks, obligations, and goals, you will automatically work in a much more effective manner. If you brake your rules, pick it right back up again and get to it. Complaining or explaining serves no purpose.

No one will hold you accountable, when you work for yourself.

Implementing your own rules will empower you to hold yourself accountable.

3rd Doctrine:
Control Your Unconscious Mind

The spiritual capitalist understands that humans are mainly guided by their unconscious mind. The vast majority of our actions and thoughts are the result of our unconscious reactions to life's stimuli. This is the very meaning of subliminal: it's unknown to us.

This is by no means an idea that only belongs to the new age community. Neuroscience has long since confirmed it, but the average person, and even most psychologists, widely ignores it. Most people naively believe that they know the ins and outs of their own minds.

Some say that 95% of our actions are guided by the unconscious. It's probably not reasonable to attach a set numeric value to it, but things to which we are completely oblivious and that are out of our control are what largely govern us. But here's the thing: even though we don't have direct access to the unconscious, we can use clever methods to manipulate it. And that is exactly what the spiritual capitalist does.

But first, let me explain why this is important.

Childhood dreams are wild and unrestrained. As we age, our dreams tend to change in tandem with our life experiences. We call childhood dreams far-fetched, but adult dreams ambitious. In reality, this is a reflection of adjusted expectations. In other words: we start setting goals that we think are realistic. Unfortunately, this also means that there is an underlying expectancy of failure in the domain in which we originally wanted to succeed. That's essentially the reason we changed our goals. We lowered the bar.

I've lived many lives, so to speak. I've lived on two continents; I've traveled the world. I've worked at the very bottom of the pyramid, in the middle, and I'm now making my way to the top, working for myself only. I know people from all walks of life, and from all over the globe. I've experienced love and loss, life and death. I've fought with swords, and with bills and partners. I've dreamed of being in movies, and I've been in movies. I've struggled and laughed and hated life and loved it. I've found the truth and realized that it wasn't the truth. I've devoted myself to people and causes and Gods and jobs, only to realize that I needed to take a different path through life. I've cleaned offices and restrooms, I've worked with mentally challenged criminals, I've been in the army, I've been a sailor, I've gambled, I've written short stories and poetry, I've played the piano, I've played computer games, I've played the markets. I've taken a degree, I've written a thesis, I've taken another degree, I've run failed companies, I've made and lost friends, I've moved away from everything I knew and started a new life. I've had many emotional and professional identities.

The sum of it all constitutes my understanding of the world.

However, many of these life experiences *could* easily have led me to adjust my expectations downwards, and thus also my level of ambition. After having settled in Los Angeles, I realized that I was an attractive candidate for many corporations, given that I'm a trilingual double graduate degree holder. I was headhunted for positions with some of the world's largest companies and, for a brief moment, it was tempting to take that route. When I was invited to interview with Google, I intuitively turned down the offer, no second thoughts. I knew that this road would never lead to me becoming an emperor.

In order to make sure that you don't adjust your level of ambition to fit your life experiences, you must develop an impenetrable sense of self-worth and the habit of visualizing the future you want. Not the future you think you can have, but the future you *actually want.*

You need to get in the habit of seeing things happening, that haven't happened yet.

People have tried to program the unconscious, or subconscious – as Freud initially called it – for more than a decade. In Los Angeles, many people practice visualization. They sometimes refer to it as manifestation, or *the law of attraction*, as it was dubbed in *The Secret,* but it's essentially the same thing. It has become an entire industry. In fact, as I was writing this very chapter on a rooftop in Hollywood, I overheard a young woman selling a manifestation course to a client on the phone. I cannot rule out that I manifested her.

Although the new age community has embraced and promoted the law of attraction for decades, many people outside this community use such techniques, and science has provided abundant evidence that visualization techniques have a multitude of very real benefits.

The brain simply doesn't distinguish between real or imagined memories. Whether you want to look at it as something supernatural is completely up to you, but there are scientifically observed benefits from visualization practices.

They:

1. Enable people to overwrite pre-existing limiting beliefs.

2. Improve performance in work, sports, and many other disciplines.

3. Increase muscle mass in people visualizing weight-lifting.

4. Increase muscle mass even more in people visualizing *and* lifting weights.

5. Have been used by athletes since the 1970s to increase performance.

6. Remove fear of specific situations and scenarios.

7. Accelerate learning of new skills.

8. Build self-confidence.

Note: At least one study has been conducted to disprove the benefits of visualization practices. The main finding of this study was that participants who imagined their dreams already fulfilled had less energy. It was therefore concluded that their goals would be harder to achieve. I am highly critical of this study and its design. Thirsty participants were basically asked to imagine drinking water, which led to decreased energy. The study explored participant reactions to basic pressing needs left unfulfilled, which has almost zero relation to the fulfillment of long-term goals, so I question the usefulness and validity of these results.

There's no reason for me to describe a specific visualization ritual here. You'll easily be able to find one online. Just keep in mind that you must implement a rule for when and how you practice it. Consistency is king. The potential benefits from visualization practices are obvious, but you can't spend hours each day imagining things if it holds you back from actually doing them. It's a supplement to the two first doctrines, not an end-all solution. This is another thing that separates the spiritual capitalist from the average person (and the average capitalist). We know that sitting and thinking about something does not make it magically manifest. But we also know that some things can be helped along by spiritual practices, such as visualization. We have our priorities straight.

There is one crucial error that many visualization and law of attraction coaches commit. Repeating your ultimate dream over and over again does not bring you closer to it, *if you don't believe in it*. In fact, if you repeatedly write down some goal, hum it as a mantra, say it over and over again, but you don't really believe in it, then that may be what you end up reinforcing: your non-belief in it. That will make the exercise yield just the opposite of what you wanted, essentially programming your unconscious for failure. So don't listen to self-taught manifestation gurus, but find a simple practice that works, and make sure that what you're trying to visualize is actually conceivable to you.

Some people prefer using affirmation practices instead of visualization or hypnosis techniques. Affirmation is a practice that involves saying bold positive statements about a desired future, as if they were already true. Affirmation practices are also based on the brain's inability to distinguish between fantasy and reality, and the reasons and ways in which they work are therefore very similar to what I already explained.

Again, I need to urge caution: there's a reason an affirmation is called an affirmation. It's something you already know in your core; not something that you don't believe. Simply wishing is not enough. Desperation doesn't reinforce anything but desperation.

For this reason, I encourage you to start using visualization techniques, and only transition into affirmations, once you feel 100% comfortable and self-confident; when you *know* that your dreams will come to fruition.

I cannot tell you how many times I've heard people say affirmations that they clearly didn't believe in. I truly believe this can be very damaging, so be mindful to only use affirmations that you can actually see happening. If you keep your focus on things that you're already working on (typically your mid-term goals), this will often be much easier.

The main benefit we get through programming our unconscious is an automatic adjustment of our responses, reactions, actions, and thoughts. They will be geared to handle the success the mind thinks you're already experiencing.

A few years ago, I decided to quit smoking. My wife told me that the hypnosis institute in LA was offering free sessions, so I thought I'd go there to ease the transition into becoming a non-smoker. During the first session, I realized that I didn't really need help to quit smoking, since I had already decided to do so. I therefore collaborated with the hypnotist to reinforce my motivation and self-discipline. I left my hypnosis sessions feeling empowered, and with an indefinable feeling that things I touched were growing, and that I was going to change the world.

You may benefit from seeing a hypnotist or listening to a guided visualization exercise, but ultimately I suggest that you implement the habit of visualization when you lie in your bed, ready to sleep. I do that every night, and I believe it primes my unconscious for high-performance the subsequent day. It's also simply a pleasant way to drift away.

The law of attraction is not a law, but there's a reason it took the world by storm. The hidden truth here is that our brain widely doesn't distinguish between real and imagined events. We can therefore fool it into believing whatever we want "it" to believe.

As you know, bullets lose height, the further they fly. You need to aim extremely high, if you want to hit anything of value. If you don't control your unconscious, other people and random forces will. Use the second doctrine to implement a consistent but not too time-consuming visualization or affirmation practice.

The Essence of Spiritual Capitalism

Most successful people describe themselves as high-performance individuals. Thousands of books have been written on high-performance practices, and you could spend tens of thousands of hours reading them all. The first time I heard about high-performance individuals, I remember thinking:

"Why would I want to be high-performing, when I don't know what to perform?"

This is the true beauty of spiritual capitalism. Following the doctrines will automatically force you to uncover what it is you need to do, and how to do it. If you follow the doctrines meticulously for at least six months, you will be well on your way to achieving your biggest goals. I guarantee you that. The doctrines will automatically transform you into a high-performing individual. If you follow them, that is.

Why isn't everybody following the doctrines already? To be perfectly honest, not everyone is cut out to do so. To many people, perhaps especially younger people, the entrepreneur life sounds exciting and summons images of fast cars, tropical islands, lots of sex, excitement, and gourmet food. The reality is that all those things are rewards that wait in the distant future. My wealth and success has certainly enabled me to do all those things, but had I done so, I would've lost track of my ultimate goal: building an empire.

Spiritual capitalists are not in it for the quick fix, we're in it for the empire.

To me, the real attraction is freedom. Not freedom to travel to a tropical island and unwind – I can do that once or twice a year with any corporate job – but freedom to pursue just about any aspiration. It's the freedom of choices. It's about having opportunities, and the longer you keep at it, the more doors will open, and the more of an impact you'll be able to make. It basically comes down to a single choice: that you will now allocate all your available time to work for yourself and put everything else on the sideline. Success comes at a cost and, as I mentioned above, most people are looking for an easy solution.

You will need practical knowledge beyond the doctrines of power and money. You need to learn how to sell, how to collaborate with people, how to find a great team, how to use other people's resources, how to manage money, how to find the right company structure, how to do online marketing, and many other things. However, as I stated in the first chapter, I didn't do any of these things even remotely right, but I've had tremendous success nonetheless. Worrying about things that may happen in the future will only hold you back.

This is the strength of the doctrines. If followed religiously, they *will* bring you success, even if you do everything else wrong. Think of it this way: the fact that employers are willing to pay you money for your time, tells you that your time is worth more than they pay you. Otherwise, they wouldn't profit from hiring you in the first place.

Once you experience the initial dose of success, you are naturally forced to deal with all the other aspects of running a business (or empire) successfully. You simply have no choice. And that's my secret sauce: we all do what we have to do, and most people don't feel like they have to do anything. The first doctrine of spiritual capitalism forces you to hold yourself accountable.

The essence of spiritual capitalism is that *you* take control over the forces that used to be out of your control. Once you've set things in motion, you have no choice but to follow through, and it'll be much easier, since you have already primed your unconscious to do so.

This is not a reckless approach to business.

It is *the only* way the average person can rise to power.

SPIRITUAL CAPITALISM

www.ingramcontent.com/pod-product-compliance
Lightning Source LLC
Chambersburg PA
CBHW020548220526
45463CB00006B/2232